Contents

T0346013

Chapter 13. Life on the Farm—Iowa Style   102

Chapter 14. New Inventions Bring Change   112

Chapter 15. Business and Industry in Iowa   121

Chapter 16. World War I and Hard Times After   127

Chapter 17. Depression, Changing Times, and World War II   133

Chapter 18. The Story Continues   142

To the Teacher

This TEACHER'S GUIDE, for IOWA PAST TO PRESENT, was written to assist elementary and middle school teachers in developing effective lessons in Iowa history. It is intended to be a starting point from which other activity ideas may grow and develop.

Each chapter of this guide corresponds to a chapter of the textbook and provides the following helps for instruction.

Content Objectives: Summarizes the most important concepts of the chapter and is based upon the Iowa history benchmarks developed by the State Historical Society of Iowa.

Vocabulary to Know: Identifies specific words that may be unfamiliar to students but pivotal to an understanding of the content.

People to Identify: Points out people of particular importance.

For Further Study: Provides additional classroom activity ideas, field trip suggestions, and sources of supplementary information to enhance the topic of study. These are, in general, more challenging activities to extend the lesson for able learners.

References: Lists sources of the primary material used in the text and suggestions for further reading.

Activities: Describes each one in detail and lists them in increasing order of complexity and demands on time. The first activities can easily be accomplished within one lesson period. The later ones are more appropriate for middle schools or those classes that study Iowa history throughout the year. The activities include references to study skills and procedures for the teacher. Necessary instructional materials (transparencies, student handouts) are also listed.

Primary Source Materials: Provides the full version of the primary materials used in the text. Teachers may be interested to read the uncut version and to share it with some students.

The textbook and teacher's guide contain a wealth of text material and teaching activities. With the current demands on school curricula, teachers may select certain portions of the text to teach in depth and others to cover more lightly or not teach at all.

The following alternatives may prove helpful when planning the Iowa history curriculum.

Iowa's Political History. Give special emphasis to the following chapters:

1. The Changing Land
3. Many Flags over Iowa
7. A Nation Divided
9. Providing a Government
16. World War I and Hard Times After
17. Depression, Changing Times, and World War II

Iowa's Ethnic Heritage. Give special emphasis to the following chapters:

2. American Indians: The Earliest People in Iowa
8. Settlers from Many Lands
12. Experiments in Community Living

Iowa's Agricultural and Business Heritage. Give special emphasis to the following chapters:

4. Pioneers on the Prairie
5. Pioneer Life on the Prairie
6. Rivers, Trails, and Train Tracks
13. Life on the Farm—Iowa Style
14. New Inventions Bring Changes
15. Business and Industry in Iowa
18. The Story Continues

Iowa's Educational and Religious Heritage. Give special emphasis to the following chapters:

10. Schools for a New State
11. Keeping Faith on the Frontier

SPECIAL ELEMENTS OF THE TEXTBOOK

Features included to supplement the text are printed on a light gray background to distinguish them from the general narrative.

A black box and thin vertical line indicate quotations, such as letters, diaries, and government papers. Ellipsis points (...) are inserted when this primary material has been shortened. This concept should be explained to the students.

Throughout the text, interesting "voices of the time" are highlighted in the margin.

1 The Changing Land

CONTENT OBJECTIVES

Following the completion of the readings and activities for this chapter, students will have acquired the following understandings:

a. Through the study of rocks and other natural features, geologists are able to create a history of Iowa's physical characteristics.
b. Several glaciers covered Iowa at various times in the ancient past.
c. Iowa's rich topsoil is a product of the thick grasses that have lived and died on the prairies for centuries.

VOCABULARY TO KNOW

Dust Bowl	limestone
fossil	loess
geologist	prairie
glaciation, glacier	sandstone
gypsum	

FOR FURTHER STUDY

1. Visit one of the many county conservation facilities across the state that provide nature displays where samples of Iowa's soil and natural vegetation may be viewed.
2. Encourage students to do research on the glacial coverings that blanketed Iowa for many centuries. Students could develop a series of maps illustrating glacial activity in Iowa during the Ice Age.
3. Invite a local resident to visit the class to recount what life was like during the days of the Dust Bowl. In addition, have students interview people in the community who remember this era. Provide class time for students to share their findings.

REFERENCES

Bonney, Margaret, ed. "Natural Resources." *The Goldfinch* 5, no. 3 (February 1984). Iowa City: State Historical Society of Iowa.

Cooper, Tom C., ed. *Iowa's Natural Heritage.* Iowa Academy of Science and the Iowa Natural Heritage Foundation, 1982.

Kurtz, Carl. *A Practical Guide To Prairie Reconstruction.* Iowa City: University of Iowa Press, 2001.

Lea, Lt. Albert M. *Notes on the Wisconsin Territory Particularly with Reference to the Iowa District or Black Hawk Purchase.* H. S. Tanner, Shakespeare Buildings, Philadelphia, Pennsylvania, 1836, pp. 11-12. Reprinted as *The Book that Gave to Iowa its Name.* Iowa City: State Historical Society of Iowa, 1935.

Swaim, Ginalie, ed. "Digging into Prehistoric Iowa." *The Goldfinch* 7, no. 1 (September 1985). Iowa City: State Historical Society of Iowa.

Activity 1-1: DEFINING HISTORY

Skills. Working in small groups

Materials. A copy of transparency 1-1

Procedure

1. Introduce the lesson by directing students to think about a definition of history. Divide the class into small groups of 3 or 4 students to write a definition of history. When students have had adequate time to complete their definitions, discuss their responses.

2. Project transparency 1-1. Read and discuss the ten definitions of history.

3. Conclude the lesson by comparing and contrasting student definitions with those on transparency 1-1.

DEFINING HISTORY

History is not history unless it is the truth.
—*Abraham Lincoln*

History does not usually make real sense until long afterward.
—*Bruce Catton*

History repeats itself because no one was listening the first time.
—*Anonymous*

History is not the accumulation of facts, but the relation of them.
—*Lytton Strachey*

To be ignorant of what happened before you were born is to be ever a child.
—*Cicero*

History repeats itself. That's one of the things wrong with history.
—*Clarence Darrow*

Life can only be understood backward, but it must be lived forward.
—*Soren Kierkegaard*

The supreme purpose of history is a better world.
—*Herbert Hoover*

History teaches everything including the future.
—*Alphonse de Lamartine*

History is something that happens to other people.
—*Anonymous*

Activity 1-2: DESCRIBING THE IOWA PRAIRIE

Skills. Interpreting primary source materials

Materials. Lt. Albert Lea's account of the Iowa District (in text), student copies of handout 1-2

Procedure

1. Distribute copies of handout 1-2. Explain to students that Lt. Albert M. Lea wrote his description of the Iowa prairie after surveying eastern Iowa in 1835. Note that the new territory was variously viewed by those who explored it. Some thought the prairie rich and inviting; others saw it as barren and desert like.

2. Read the Lea paragraphs (in text) aloud while students follow along. Provide time for students to complete the questions in handout 1-2.

3. Conclude the lesson by discussing Lt. Lea's representation of Iowa. He was obviously interested in describing Iowa in the most positive light to attract newcomers to the state.

Name _____

DESCRIBING THE IOWA PRAIRIE

Directions. Use the information in the text to answer the following questions.

1. What part of present-day Iowa did Lieutenant Lea describe? _____

_____

_____

2. What natural resources did Lea list? _____

_____

_____

3. Why did Lea present Iowa in such a positive light? _____

_____

_____

_____

_____

_____

_____

_____

_____

Activity 1-3: TIMELINE

Skills. Determining length and scale for a timeline

Materials. Paper for constructing a classroom timeline

Procedure

1. Prior to this lesson, put up the timeline in the classroom. If possible, have it span the perimeter of the room, beginning with 10,000 B.C. (the close of the glacial age in Iowa) and extending to the present.

2. Introduce this lesson by reviewing with students that scientists believe people have lived in Iowa for approximately 12,000 years, and the last glaciers receded only 12,000 years ago. Have students mark the beginning of the classroom timeline with the year 10,000 B.C. Next have students mark off each thousand-year segment by measuring the length of the timeline and dividing by 12 to find the length of each 1000-year segment. (It may be advisable to expand the last two centuries to provide space for more detail.)

3. Review the following information from the text:

• Around 10,000 B.C. the last glacier retreated from Iowa. The temperature grew gradually warmer. Hardwood trees replaced forests of fir trees. Later, as the climate grew warmer still, grasslands grew where hardwood trees had grown.

• Around 4,000 years ago the climate began to moderate. Trees began to grow again along streams and rivers. Since then the trees and grasses have played tug-of-war over the land as temperatures and rainfall have fluctuated.

• Have students mark the timeline to reflect these periods of climatic change.

4. Conclude the lesson by noting that the timeline will serve as a classroom reference, and new information will be added periodically. In addition, the majority of the study will focus on the final timeline section representing the last 200 years.

Activity 1-4: A JOKE FROM THE SEA

This story of an unusual use of Iowa gypsum has long been well known in the state. The teacher may wish to relate or read it as a background to the illustration in the text.

As American settlers moved west, they often found items from Indian peoples who lived there long ago. The settlers were curious about those who had lived on the land before them and wanted to know where the Indians came from and how they lived. This gave a man named George Hull an idea for a fraud that made him a lot of money.

Shortly after the Civil War, Hull bought a large block of gypsum in Fort Dodge and shipped it to Chicago in a large wooden crate. Only a few people knew that he had bought it, and he kept his purchase a secret. In Chicago, a stonecutter began chipping away at the block of gypsum until he carved it into the figure of a man. Working by himself and keeping the project a secret, he finished the statue and shipped it to Cardiff, New York. There it was buried in a field of a farmer, a friend of Hull's who was in on the scheme.

After a time, the farmer declared that he needed to dig a new well. He hired workers and told them where to dig—in the very spot where the statue had been buried. Of course, the workers knew nothing about the statue. When they found it, they were very excited, thinking that they had found a strange relic from an ancient time. The farmer pretended to be very excited also. He did not tell the workers that the statue was a big chunk of gypsum from Fort Dodge, Iowa.

News of the discovery spread quickly. An ancient carving had been found! It was nearly ten feet long and solid rock. Newspapers printed long stories about the discovery, and people by the hundreds came to see it. They paid fifty cents each to look at the wonderful discovery. Even some famous scientists were fooled. They examined it and reported that it was indeed an ancient statue. The carving became known as the Cardiff Giant.

Finally, a newspaper reporter discovered the true story. The giant was a fake. Someone found the record of Hull's purchase of the gypsum in Fort Dodge, and there was also the record of the shipment to Chicago. Some people who had been fooled were angry but others thought it was a great joke. Regardless, Hull made a lot of money.

Today, the Cardiff Giant lies peacefully in a museum in Cooperstown, New York. A copy has been made for a museum in Fort Dodge. That joke from Iowa's past began millions of years ago. Gypsum is one of the gifts from the shallow sea that once washed across the state.

PRIMARY SOURCE MATERIAL: Lt. Albert Lea's Account of the Iowa District (unabridged)

The general appearance of the country is one of great beauty. It may be represented as one grand rolling prairie, along one side of which flows the mightiest river in the world, and through which numerous navigable streams pursue their devious way towards the ocean. In every part of the whole District, beautiful rivers and creeks are to be found, whose transparent waters are perpetually renewed by the springs from which they flow. Many of these streams are connected with lakes; and hence their supply of water is remarkable uniform throughout the seasons. All these rivers, creeks, and lakes, are skirted by woods, often several miles in width, affording shelter from intense cold or heat to the animals that may there take refuge from the contiguous prairies. These woods also afford the timber necessary for building houses, fences, and boats. Though probably three-fourths of the District is without trees, yet so conveniently and admirably are the water and the woods distributed throughout, that nature appears to have made an effort to arrange them in the most desirable manner possible. Where there is no water, isolated groves are frequently found to break the monotony of the prairie, or to afford the necessary timber for the enclosure of the farmer. No part of the District is probably more than three miles from good timber, and hence it is scarcely any where necessary to build beyond the limits of the woods to be convenient to farming lands the most distant from them, as the trouble of hauling the timber necessary for farming purposes, a distance of one, two or three miles, is trifling. Taking this District all in all, for convenience of navigation, water, fuel, and timber; for richness of soil; for beauty of appearance; and for pleasantness of climate, it surpasses any portion of the United States with which I am acquainted.

Could I present to the mind of the reader that view of this country that is now before my eyes, he would not deem my assertion unfounded. He would see the broad Mississippi with its ten thousand islands, flowing gently and lingeringly along one entire side of this District, as if in regret at leaving so delightful a region; he would see half a doze before my eyes, he would not deem my assertion unfounded. He would see the broad Mississippi with its ten thousand islands, flowing gently and lingeringly along one entire side of this District, as if in regret at leaving so delightful a region; he would see half a dozen navigable rivers taking their sources in distant regions, and gradually accumulating their waters as they glide steadily along through this favoured region to pay their tribute to the great "Father of Waters"; he would see innumerable creeks and rivulets meandering through rich pasturages, where now the domestic ox has taken the place of the untamed bison; he would see here and there neat groves of oak, and elm, and walnut, half shading half concealing beautiful little lakes, that mirror back their waiving branches; he would see neat looking prairies of two or three miles in extent, and apparently enclosed by woods on all sides, and along the borders of which are ranged the neat hewed log cabins of the emigrants with their herds luxuriating on the native grass; he would see villages springing up, as by magic, along the banks of the rivers, and liberally dispensed.

FROM: Lea, Lt. Albert M. *Notes on the Wisconsin Territory Particularly with Reference to the Iowa District or Black Hawk Purchase.* H. S. Tanner, Shakespeare Buildings, Philadelphia, Pennsylvania, 1836, pp. 11-12. Reprinted as *The Book that Gave to Iowa its Name.* Iowa City: State Historical Society of Iowa, 1935.

2 American Indians

THE EARLIEST PEOPLE IN IOWA

CONTENT OBJECTIVES

Following the completion of the readings and activities for this chapter, students will have acquired the following understandings:

a. Archaeologists believe that people first arrived in what is today Iowa approximately 12,000 years ago. These people were the ancestors of the American Indians of today.
b. The first Iowans used the earth's resources for food, clothing, and shelter.
c. The federal government tried to control American Indians through treaties and forced land sales. As a result, tribes frequently moved into and out of Iowa.
d. The Mesquakies, one of the most enduring Iowa tribes, still live on their settlement near Tama.

VOCABULARY TO KNOW

ancestors

archaeologist

mound builders

nomads

tributary rivers

PEOPLE AND PLACES TO IDENTIFY

Black Hawk

Ioway

Keokuk

Mesquakie

Mississippi River

Nicolas Perrot

Sauk

Saukenuk

Sioux

Tama

FOR FURTHER STUDY

1. A tour of the Effigy Mounds National Monument near McGregor is a rewarding and educational experience.

2. A visit to the Living History Farms near Des Moines will help students better understand Iowa's Indian populations.

3. A visit to a special festival, such as the Tama Indian Powwow held each August, will provide students with a firsthand cultural experience of Indian origin.

4. Teachers may also want to take advantage of local citizens of Indian descent. These individuals can share customs and traditions with students, which will add a practical dimension to the study of this important group of people.

5. *From Ackley to Zwingle: A Collection of the Origins of Iowa Place Names,* Second Edition, Harold E. Dilts (Iowa State University Press, Ames, Iowa, 1993) provides an interesting explanation of the origins of Iowa's county names. These names, many of which are of Indian origin, can be used as anecdotal information to increase students' interest in the study of their state.

REFERENCES

Anderson, Duane. *Eastern Iowa Prehistory.* Ames: Iowa State University Press, 1981.

Bonney, Margaret, ed. "Indians of Iowa." *The Goldfinch* 3, no.4 (April 1982). Iowa City: State Historical Society of Iowa.

Encyclopedia of Iowa Indians: Tribes, Nations and People of The Woodlands Areas. St. Clair Shores, MI: Somerset Publishers, 1998.

Hagan, William. "The Sacs and Foxes of the Mississippi Valley." In *Patterns and Perspectives in Iowa History,* Dorothy Schwieder, ed. Ames: Iowa State University Press, 1973.

Schilz, Thomas F. and Jodye, L.D. "The Rise and Fall of the Indian Fur Trade Along the Missouri and Des Moines Rivers 1700-1820." *The Annals of Iowa* 49, nos. 1 and 2 (Summer/Fall 1987). Iowa City: State Historical Society of Iowa.

Schoolcraft, Henry R. *Information Respecting the History, Condition and Prospects of the Indian Tribes of the United States,* III. Philadelphia: Lippincott, Grambo and Company, 1853, 256-58.

Schwieder, Dorothy. "Native Americans in Iowa." In *Iowa: The Middle Land.* Ames: Iowa State University Press, 1996, Chapter 1.

Smith, Michael C. "You Gotta Know the Territory; Material Culture from Territorial Iowa." *The Palimpsest* 69, no. 2 (Summer 1988). Iowa City: State Historical Society of Iowa.

Swaim, Ginalie ed. "'Clothe Yourself in Fine Apparel': Mesquakie Costume in Word, Image, and Artifact." *The Palimpsest* 72, no. 2 (Summer 1991). Iowa City: State Historical Society of Iowa.

Torrence, Gaylord. "A Mesquakie Drawing." *The Palimpsest* 69, no. 2 (Summer 1988). Iowa City: State Historical Society of Iowa.

Vogel, Virgil J. *Iowa Place Names of Indian Origin.* Ames: Iowa State University Press, 1983.

Activity 2-1: MIGRATION OF THE IOWAY TRIBE

Skills. Map Reading

Materials. Schoolcraft map and account of Ioway migrations (in textbook), student copies of handout 2-1 (optional)

Procedure

1. Introduce the lesson by reviewing the textbook material on the Ioway Indians in the textbook.

2. Locate the map of the Ioway Indians in textbook *or* distribute copies of handout 2-1. Emphasize that this selection was based on the recollections of an Ioway Indian. Have students follow along on their maps as the material on their migrations is read to the class. Using the information in the last paragraph, have students estimate the approximate date of the writing of this selection.

3. Conclude the lesson by having students locate and, if possible, draw the present-day state boundaries on their maps. Discuss the great amount of territory the Ioway Indians covered in this segment of their history. Consider some reasons for these migrations (availability of food, supply of bark and firewood, etc.).

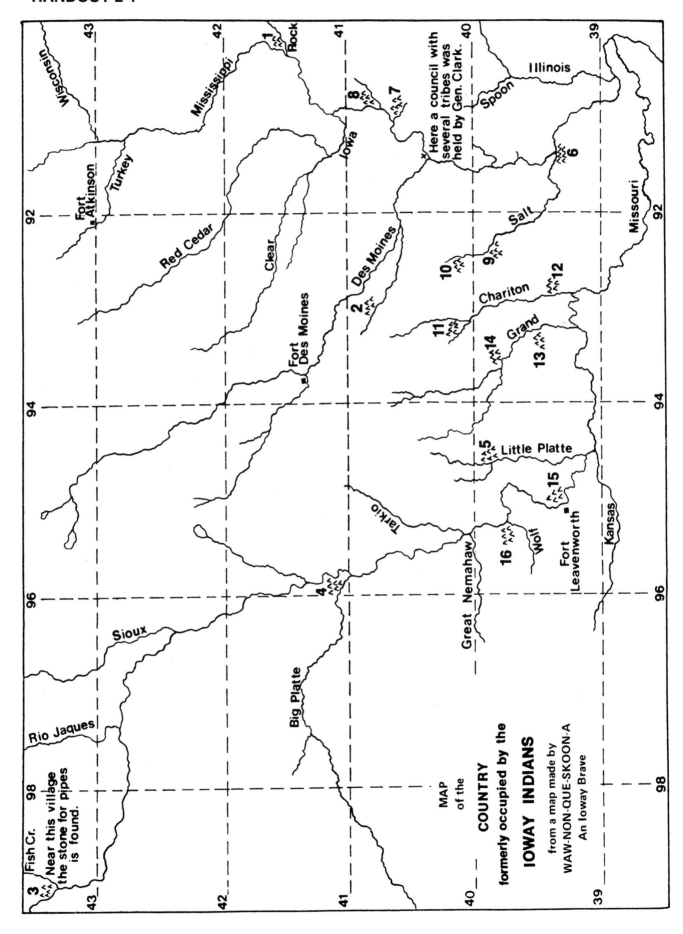

MAP
of the

COUNTRY
formerly occupied by the

IOWAY INDIANS

from a map made by
WAW-NON-QUE-SKOON-A
An Ioway Brave

Activity 2-2: INDIAN PLACE NAMES

Skills. Identifying specific counties on Iowa maps

Materials. Student copies of handout 2-2, resource materials containing information on Iowa Indians, Iowa road maps (optional)

Procedure

1. Introduce the lesson by reviewing with students that Iowa was first inhabited by various American Indian groups such as the Ioway, the Sioux, Winnebagos, the Otos, and the Omahas. Have students name several of these groups.

2. Distribute copies of handout 2-2. Have students skim the map for county names of Indian origin. The following list identifies county names and the tribe with which each is associated. Students will be able to identify others as well.

Appanoose—Sauk	Pocahontas—Powhatan
Black Hawk—Sauk	Pottawattamie—an Indian tribe
Cherokee—an Indian tribe	Tama—Mesquakie
Chickasaw—an Indian tribe	Wapello—Mesquakie
Keokuk—Sauk	Winnebago—an Indian tribe
Mahaska—Ioway	Winneshiek—Winnebago
Osceola—Seminole	

3. Compile a list of county names on the blackboard. Using the textbook and other resource materials (see references), have students identify the tribe with which each name is associated.

4. If time permits, have students compile a list of town and city names of Indian origin using the Iowa road maps.

5. Culminate the lesson by posting the county and town names on charts to be displayed in the room.

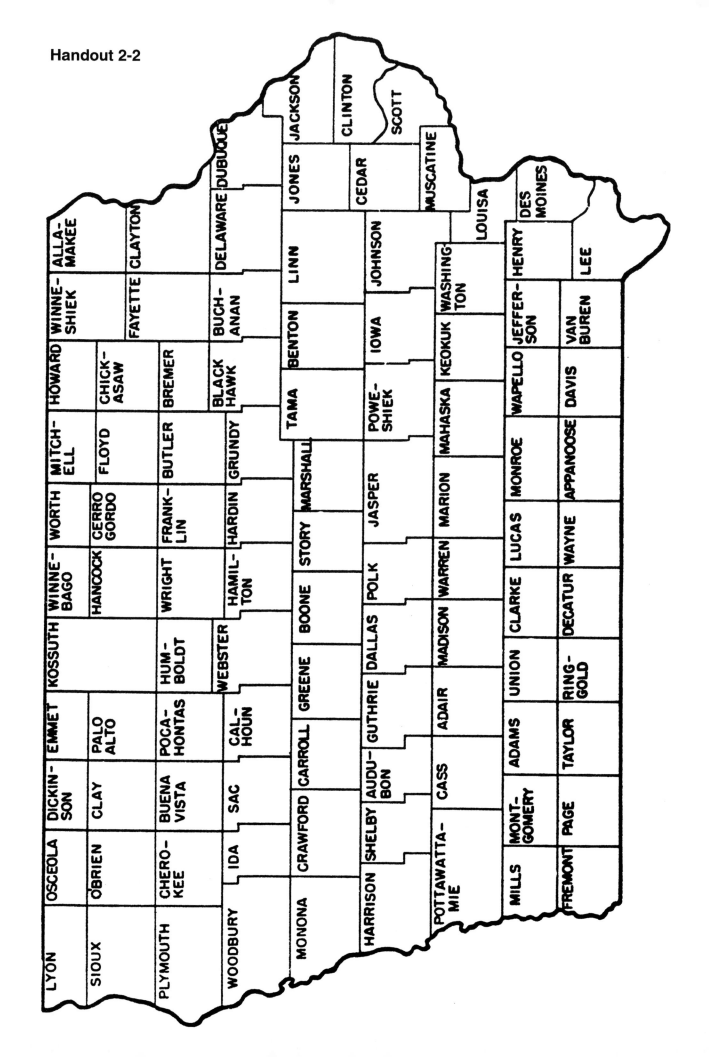

The original outlines of the Indian map were drawn in the rough by Waw-non-que-skoon-a, an Iowa Indian, with a black-lead pencil on a large sheet of white paper, furnished at the mission-house on their reservation on the Kansas-Nebraska border (No. 16 on the map). It has been reduced in size, and its rigid lines adaptcd to the surveys of the public lands on the Missouri and Mississippi. The original is retained in the Indian Bureau.

The object of Waw-non-que-skoon-a was to denote the places where the Iowas had lived using the sixteen migrations which preceded their residence at their present location, the Missouri; and, in truth, it nearly exhausts their history. The marks to denote a fixed residence, are a symbol for a lodge. These are carefully preserved, with their exact relative position. Their order, as given, is also preserved by figures. Could eras be affixed to these residences, it would give entire accuracy to the modern part of their history.

As it is, it depicts some curious facts in the history of predatory and erratic tribes, showing how they sometimes crossed their own track, and demonstrates the immense distances to which they rove.

The earliest date to which their recollection extends, as indicated by location No. 1, is at the junction of Rock River with the Mississippi. This was, manifestly, in or very near Winnebago territory, and confirms the traditions of several of the Missouri tribes. ... From this point they migrated down the Mississippi to the river Des Moines and fixed themselves at No. 2, on its south fork. They next made an extraordinary migration, abandoning the Mississippi and all its upper tributaries, and ascending the Missouri to a point of land formed by a small stream, on its east shore, called by the Indians Fish Creek, which flows in from the direction of, and not far from, the celebrated Red Pipe stone quarry, on the heights of the Coteau des Prairies. No. 3.

They next descended the Missouri to the junction of the Nebraska, or Great Platte river, with that stream. No. 4. They settled on the west bank, keeping the buffalo ranges on their west. They next migrated still lower down the Missouri, and fixed themselves on the head-waters of the Little Platte river. No. 5.

From this location, when circumstances had rendered another change desirable, they returned to the Mississippi, and located themselves at the mouth of Salt river. No. 6. Here passed another period. They next ascended the Mississippi, and settled on its east bank, at the junction of a stream in the present area of Illinois. No. 7. Their next migration carried them still higher on that shore, to the junction of another stream, No. 8, which is well nigh to their original starting point at No. 1.

They receded again to the south and west, first fixing themselves on Salt river, No. 9, above their prior site, No. 6, and afterwards changing their location to its very source. No. 10. They then passed, evidently by land, to the higher forks of the river Chariton, of Missouri, No. 11, and next descended that stream to near its mouth. No. 12. The next two migrations of this tribe were to the west valley of the Grand river, and then to its forks. No. 14. Still continuing their general migrations to the south and west, they chose the east bank of the Missouri, opposite the present site of Fort Leavenworth, No. 15, and finally settled on the west bank of the Missouri, between the mouth of the Wolf and Great Namahaw, No. 16, where they now reside.

These migrations are deemed to be all of quite modern date, not exceeding the probable period to which well-known tradition could reach. They do not, it would seem, aspire to the area of their ancient residence on the lower and upper Iowa rivers, and about the region of St. Anthony's falls. ...

We are taught something by these migrations. They were probably detemined by the facility of procuring food. They relied, ever, greatly on the deer, elk, and buffalo. As these species are subject to changes, it is probable they carried the Indians with them. It is not probable that their locations were of long continuance at a place. Not over a dozen years at a location, on the average. It might be longer at some places, and less at others. This would not give a period of more than 180 years, before their arrival at their present place. Marquette found them, in 1673, at the mouth of the Des Moines. This, it is seen, was their first location.

FROM: Henry R. Schoolcraft. 1853. *Information Respecting the History, Condition and Prospects of the Indian Tribes of the United States,* III. Philadelphia: Lippincott, Grambo and Company, pp. 256-58.

Activity 2-3: THE DEATH OF BLACK HAWK

Skills. Reading and comparing primary and secondary accounts

Materials. Student copies of handouts 2-3a and 2-3b

Procedure

1. Introduce the lesson by distributing copies of handout 2-3a. Read and discuss this selection together as a class.

2. Have students turn to the account of Sarah Nossaman (handout 2-3b). Read and discuss this selection together, identifying on an Iowa map the locations she mentions.

3. After discussing the difference between a primary and secondary source, ask students to compare and contrast these two accounts of Black Hawk's death. Focus discussion on the strengths and liabilities of personal accounts of historical events.

THE DEATH OF BLACKHAWK

Following the Black Hawk War of 1832, Chief Black Hawk was put in prison for a short time, first in St. Louis and then in Virginia. When President Andrew Jackson arranged for his release, Black Hawk returned to Iowa, the land he loved. Iowa was Black Hawk's last home. He built a home along the Des Moines River in central Iowa.

Black Hawk died in October of 1838. But even in death he was not free from humiliation. During his life, Black Hawk's land had been taken by pioneer settlers moving west. Now in his death they robbed his grave. His body was dug up and plans were made to display his skull and bones like a circus sideshow. Some of Black Hawk's friends appealed to Governor Robert Lucas, who demanded that the bones be returned from Illinois to Iowa. They were placed in a Burlington museum, which burned in 1855.

SARAH NOSSAMAN'S STORY

These recollections of pioneer life were written by Sarah Welch Nossaman so that her children would have some record of her early life. She recalls her family's move to Indiana in 1831 when she was only six years old. In 1835 her family moved again to Bonaparte, Iowa, where her father built a pottery. In 1841 they moved again to Fairfield, Iowa, where she married. In 1842 Sarah and her husband moved to a new settlement near Pella, Iowa. Unfortunately, her record ends abruptly in 1844 and does not chronicle the Nossamans' later efforts at hotel-keeping and store-keeping in Pella.

On the following April the Black Hawk War broke out, and some of our neighbors were killed near us, but we were providentially spared. While the war was raging at its hottest my mother urged my father to go to Jacksonville, the county seat of Morgan County, Illinois, and get his brother, which is old Uncle Johnny Welch of this place, to come and take us down to Jacksonville where he lived. ... In 1835 my father moved to what is now Iowa, but at that time it was part of Wisconsin Territory. We settled one mile below where Bonaparte now is, in Van Buren County .We had but few neighbors, among them being old Uncle Sammy Reed and his brother Isaac, and an Indian trader by the name of Jordan. ... It was here we had for neighbors Black Hawk, Keokuk, Wapello, Hard Fish, Kishkakosh, Naseaskuk and a score of others of the Sac and Fox Indians. Here we had hard times and often went hungry. We lived there five years. ... While we lived there Black Hawk and his son were frequent visitors and often partook of my father's hospitality.

In 1837 or 1838, I don't remember which, Black Hawk died of malaria fever. One of our neighbors, Dr. James Turner, thought if he could only steal Black Hawk's head he could make a fortune out of it by taking it east and putting it on exhibition. After two weeks' watching he succeeded in getting it. Black Hawk's burial place was near old Iowaville, on the north side of the Des Moines River, under a big sugar tree. It was there Dr. Turner severed the head from the body. At the time it was done I was taking care of his sick sister-in-law, Mrs. William Turner. The doctor made his home with his brother. We knew the evening he went to steal the head and sat up to await his coming. He got in with it at four o'clock in the morning and hid it till the afternoon of the same day, when he cooked the flesh off the skull. So I can say that I am the only one now living that witnessed that sight, for it was surely a sight for me. If the rest of Black Hawk's bones were ever removed it was a good many years after his head was stolen.

The second morning after their ruler's head was stolen ten of the best Indian warriors came to William Turner's and asked for his brother, the Doctor. They were painted war style. He told them he did not know where his brother was. They told him they would give him ten days to find his brother, and if he did not find him in that time he would pay the penalty for his brother's crime. But he knew where his brother was. He was at the home of a neighbor named Robb, Uncle Tommy Robb as he was called by everyone, on the south side of the Des Moines River. But he did not want to find his brother and sent a boy to tell him to fly for Missouri, which he did. The Indians returned to Iowaville to hold council and conclude what to do, and while they were holding council William Turner and his wife made their escape in a canoe down the river. William Turner kept a little store in new Lexington. He got his neighbors to pack and send his goods after him.

But the Indians demanded their ruler's head, and for three weeks we expected an outbreak every day, but through the influence of their agent and the citizens together they gave up hostilities for a time. The whites told them they would bring Turner to justice if he could be found. The sheriff chased Turner around for awhile, which only give him the more time to get out of the way. The Turner family finally all went to St. Louis where the Doctor was found again, and to keep the Indians quiet the sheriff went to St. Louis in search of him, but he did not find him. He did not want to find him. But Turner got frightened and took Black Hawk's skull to Quincy, Illinois, and put it in the care of a doctor there for safe-keeping (I forget the doctor's name) till the Indians would get settled down, and then he intended to take it east. But when he got ready to go east with it the doctor in Quincy refused to give it up, and he did not dare to go to law about it, so after all his trouble and excitement he lost Black Hawk's skull, and not only made Turners endless trouble, but put the lives of all settlers in jeopardy for months. We lived principally on excitement and that was a poor living. But they finally got over it till all was peace and then we were happy. The doctor that had the head took it to Burlington and sold it to a museum and the museum burned down, so Black Hawk's skull is not now in existence. The Turner family were warm friends of my father's family. They stayed in St. Louis two or three years, I don't remember just how long, and they all three died with the cholera. So I am left alone to tell the story.

———————

FROM: Sarah Welch Nossaman. "Pioneering at Bonaparte and Near Pella." *Annals of Iowa* 13 (1922). 443-45.

3 Many Flags over Iowa

CONTENT OBJECTIVES

Following the completion of the readings and activities for this chapter, students will have acquired the following understandings:

a. The French, English, and Spanish claimed large sections of land in North America at various times during the 17th, 18th, and 19th centuries.
b. The land area of present-day Iowa became part of the U.S. in 1803 with the Louisiana Purchase.
c. Several exploring parties were sent to the lands west of the Mississippi to assess the possibilities for settlement.
d. Iowa became part of the United States in an orderly process provided by the Federal government, moving through district and territory status to full statehood in 1846.

VOCABULARY TO KNOW

claim   empire

colonies   Louisiana Purchase

descendants   Missouri River

PEOPLE TO IDENTIFY

Captain Meriwether Lewis   Louis Jolliet

Father Jacques Marquette   Napoleon

Julien Dubuque   Thomas Jefferson

La Salle   Zebulon Pike

Lieutenant William Clark

FOR FURTHER STUDY

1. Encourage students to consult the local courthouse deed records on a specific piece of land, such as a farm, a town lot, or school property. Deed records will indicate the name of the purchaser, date of purchase, a description of the property, and the price. These data will not only prove informative for students but will also lend interest to the study of local history.

2. Have students use a general reference on Iowa history to make large poster-size maps of the Michigan Territory (1834), the Wisconsin Territory (1836), and the Iowa Territory (1838).

REFERENCES

Sage, Leland L. "Iowaland: Indian, French, Spanish, American 1673-1803." In *A History of Iowa*. Ames: Iowa State University Press, 1974. Chapter 2.

Swaim, Ginalie, ed. "The Fur Trade." *The Goldfinch* 6, no. 2 (December 1984). Iowa City: State Historical Society of Iowa.

Wall, Joseph F. "We Occupy the Land and Organize It." In *Iowa: A Bicentennial History*. New York: W. W. Norton, 1978. Chapter 2.

Activity 3-1: LOCATING FRONTIER IOWA

Skills. Labeling, reading, and interpreting maps

Materials. Student copies of handouts 3-1a and 3-1b, classroom wall map of the United States

Procedure

1. Introduce the lesson by reviewing the national setting in 1832. Iowa was still part of the unorganized territories of the West. The quest for new western territory to settle intensified as land in the East became increasingly expensive. Treaty negotiations and resettlement attempts between the federal government and the various western Indian tribes often resulted in conflict and bloodshed. One of these conflicts, often remembered as Black Hawk's War, resulted in the opening of a portion of Iowa to pioneer settlement in 1833.

2. Distribute copies of handouts 3-1a and 3-1b. Read and discuss the directions together as a class and provide time for students to complete the questions.

3. Conclude the lesson by discussing the handout questions and contrasting Iowa's place on the frontier in 1832 with Iowa's place today in the United States.

Name _____

LOCATING FRONTIER IOWA

Directions. Using the classroom wall map of the United States, complete the following items on your 1832 map of the United States. Then answer questions 1-9.

Label and shade the Atlantic and Pacific oceans, the Gulf of Mexico, and the Great Lakes. Label the Mississippi, Missouri, and Ohio rivers. Label the states. Mark the western boundary of the United States in 1832.

1. What state was on the eastern boundary of present-day Iowa?

   _____

2. What state was on the southern boundary of present-day Iowa?

   _____

3. What states or territories formed the western boundary of the United States in 1832?

   _____

4. What territory was Iowa part of in 1832? _____

5. How many states were in the Union in 1832? _____

6. List the states west of the Mississippi River in 1832. _____

   _____

7. How many states are west of the Mississippi River today? _____

8. Describe Iowa's location in relation to the centers of United States population in 1832.

   _____

   _____

9. Describe Iowa's location in relation to the centers of United States population today.

   _____

   _____

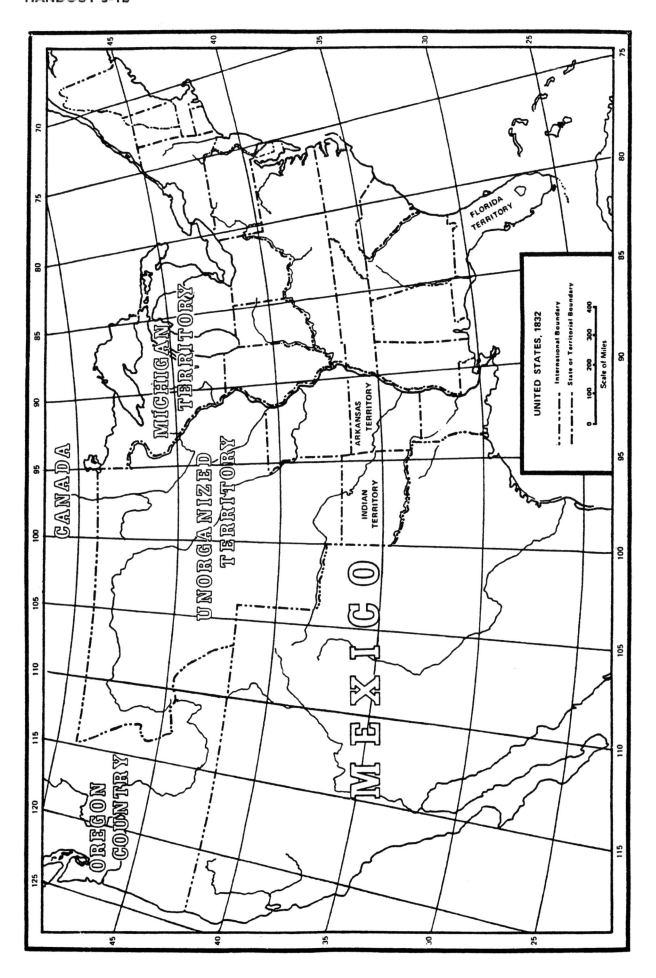

Activity 3-2: DISCOVERING FRONTIER IOWA

Skills. Interpreting maps

Materials. Lea's map of part of the Wisconsin Territory, 1836 (in text), student copies of handout 3-2

Procedure

1. Introduce the lesson by discussing the following information. In 1835 Colonel Stephen W. Kearney led three companies of soldiers on a march through eastern Iowa. They were in search of a location for a possible fort. One of the men was Lt. Albert M. Lea. In addition to keeping a diary of his experiences, and writing a book describing Iowa in 1835, he made a map of the area.

2. Distribute copies of handout 3-2. Read the directions together and provide time for students to compete the questions.

3. Conclude the lesson by discussing student responses.

DISCOVERING FRONTIER IOWA

Directions. Find places in Iowa according to a map prepared by the surveyor, Lieutenant Albert M. Lea, U.S. Dragoons, in 1836. Use the information on the map to answer the following questions:

1. What Iowa towns are shown on the territorial map? _____

_____

_____

2. What Iowa counties are shown on the territorial map? _____

_____

_____

3. How were the Iowa counties in 1836 different from Iowa counties today? _____

_____

_____

4. List the Indian villages shown on the territorial map. _____

_____

_____

5. What mineral resources are shown on the territorial map? _____

_____

6. What part of Iowa was open to settlement by U.S. citizens? _____

_____

7. Which Indian tribes were living in the part of Iowa shown on the territorial map? ____

_____

_____

Activity 3-3: WHO'S WHO IN IOWA'S MARCH TO STATEHOOD

Skills. Skimming written material for specific information

Materials. Ten 3"x6" name tags with the following names printed on them: Father Jacques Marquette, Louis Jolliet, La Salle, Julien Dubuque, President Thomas Jefferson, Napoleon, Captain Meriwether Lewis, William Clark, Zebulon Pike, and Lt. Albert M. Lea

Procedure

1. Begin the lesson by briefly reviewing the events which led to Iowa's statehood:

   a. Louisiana, of which Iowa was a part, was first claimed by France.
   b. The English did not honor the French claims and war ensued.
   c. France then secretly gave its lands west of the Mississippi to Spain.
   d. In 1800 this land was returned to France as Napoleon tried to create an empire in North America.
   e. In 1803 Louisiana was sold by France to the United States for $15,000,000.
   f. The federal government sent out expeditions to assess the possibilities of this newly acquired land to the west.
   g. Iowa was first a part of Michigan Territory, then Wisconsin Territory, and finally Iowa Territory before becoming a state in 1846.

2. Display the ten name tags in the front of the room. Provide time for students to skim the chapter, identifying and discussing each person's contribution to the saga of Iowa's settlement. Have the class select five of the characters for the Who's Who game.

3. Assign a different name to five student volunteers without letting the class know which character was assigned to which student. The five students stand in front of the class.

4. The class will try to identify which person has been assigned to which student by asking specific questions about the contributions of the character. If time permits, the game may be repeated using the remaining five characters.

4 Pioneers on the Prairie

CONTENT OBJECTIVES

Following the completion of the readings and activities for this chapter, students will have acquired the following understandings:

a. Most pioneer settlers came to Iowa from the eastern United States and Europe.
b. Iowa land was surveyed by the government and sold at auctions held by government land officers.
c. For most settlers, living on the prairie meant a change in farming and household practices.

VOCABULARY TO KNOW

1800s, nineteenth century	settlement
immigrant	sod house
land survey	squatter
pioneer	township
prairie	woodscraft

FOR FURTHER STUDY

1. Visit a preserved virgin prairie. Throughout Iowa, several plots have been set aside for educational purposes. Kalsow Prairie near Fort Dodge, Caylor Prairie near Spirit Lake, and the Neal Smith National Wildlife Refuge near Prairie City are available for groups to visit. Consult your county conservation board for assistance in teaching about prairie life. Many counties have nature centers set aside primarily for educational purposes.

2. Have students survey their families to discover when and from where their fam-

ilies moved to Iowa. Some students will discover that their ancestors came directly from Europe. Others will find that their families moved to Iowa from an eastern state. Have students share their findings with the class.

REFERENCES

Acton, Richard. "'Hawkeye:' What's in a Name?" *The Palimpsest* 70, no. 3 (Fall 1989). Iowa City: State Historical Society of Iowa.

1870 *Iowa State Almanac.* Explorations in Iowa History Project. Cedar Falls: Malcolm Price Laboratory School, University of Northern Iowa.

Fairchild, Ephraim G. Collection, March 1857-October 1858. Manuscript Collection. Iowa City: State Historical Society of Iowa.

Grindal, Gracia. "Linka Preus' Sketches of Iowa." *The Palimpsest* 67, no.4 (July/August 1986). Iowa City: State Historical Society of Iowa.

Kenyon, John B., and Sarah Kenyon Collection, Aug. 29, 1856-March 2, 1865, Manuscript Collection. Iowa City: State Historical Society of Iowa.

Schwieder, Dorothy. "Pioneers on the Prairie." In *Iowa: The Middle Land.* Iowa State University Press, 1996. Chapter 1.

Swaim, Ginalie, ed. "Life on the Iowa Prairies." *The Goldfinch* 7, no.2 (November 1985). Iowa City: State Historical Society of Iowa.

Activity 4-1: MIGRATION STATISTICS

Skills. Reading charts and maps

Materials. Tables of 1870 census (in text) and classroom maps of the United States and the world

Procedure

1. Find 1870 census tables in text.

2. Identify 1870 with the close of the pioneer period in Iowa. Note that the native-born population of Iowa was almost five times as great as the foreign-born population for 1870.

3. Note that about one-third of Iowa's population in 1870 was born in Iowa.

4. Have students identify and locate on the United States map the five states in which the largest number of Iowans were born.

5. Have students identify and locate on the world map the three foreign countries in which the largest number of Iowans were born.

6. Have volunteers do a survey of the students in the classroom, determining the birthplaces of the students and their immediate family members. A chart of their findings could provide a birthplace profile for the classroom.

Activity 4-2: PIONEER TRANSPORTATION

Skills. Collecting information from primary source materials

Materials. Transparency 4-2 (Fairchild letter, also in text), student copies of handout 4-2, colored transparency markers, crayons

Procedure

1. Introduce the lesson by rereading the section on pioneer transportation in the textbook.

2. Project transparency 4-2. Allow time for students to read the Fairchild letter independently or have it read aloud for the class.

3. Assign a different color to each means of transportation listed in the letter (train, wagon, walking). Using the colored transparency pens, have students take turns coming to the projector and marking the parts of the letter which refer to a means of transportation. Discuss the variety of transportation methods used.

4. Distribute copies of handout 4-2. Using crayons, have students mark the route of the travelers, color-coding the route according to the colors used on the letter.

PRIMARY SOURCE MATERIAL: LETTER OF EPHRAIM G. FAIRCHILD

Pleasant Ridge March 23, 1857

  Ever Kind and affectionate Father and Mother and all the rest of the friends. I take my pen in hand to write a few lines to you to let you know that we are all well at present and hope these few lines may find you all the same.
  I will try to tell you some thing about our journey out west. we had a very slow trip, the cars run very slow all the way from Jersey City up to Dunkirk [N.Y.] so we did not make connection with the train from their and had to stop there from 2 oclock in the afternoon until 2½ oclock Wednesday morning. then we Started for Cleveland and arrived there about noon and missed the train there again. we had to stay their till about 4 oclock in the evening. then we started for toledo and there we made connection with the wagon [train] going to chicago and there we had to stop about 4 or 5 hours longer. then we started about 9 in the evening for Dunleath [now called East Dubuque]. we arrived there about 9 or 10 on friday morning and there we met uncle Jerry. he started from home on wednesday and arrived at Dubuque on thrusday and on friday we crossed the missippia on the ice with the horses and wagon. then we started for uncle Jerrie's.
  we got as far as the 11 mild [mile] house. then we put up and in the morning we started again and went about 1 mild and broke the arm of the axel tree. then we was in a fix. no house nearer than a mild but Eliza and the children got out of the wagon and went on to the 12 mild house afoot and uncle and I unloded the things into another wagon and fixed up the wagon so as to get to the 12 mild house and there was a black smith shop and the smith thought he could fix it. so he went at it as soon as he cood and when he got it fixed it was about 2 or 3 oclock. then we started again and traveled on until night. then we put up at Ozark with a man by the name of E. West. they were verry nice people. the next morning which was sunday morning it thundred and lightened and rained quite hard untill about 9 oclock, then it stopped and about 10 uncle said he though we had better start before the river at canton got so high that it wood be dangerous. so we started and got acrost the river safe and went on home, we got to uncles about 4 oclock sunday after noon all safe and sound but mudier going I never saw in my life.

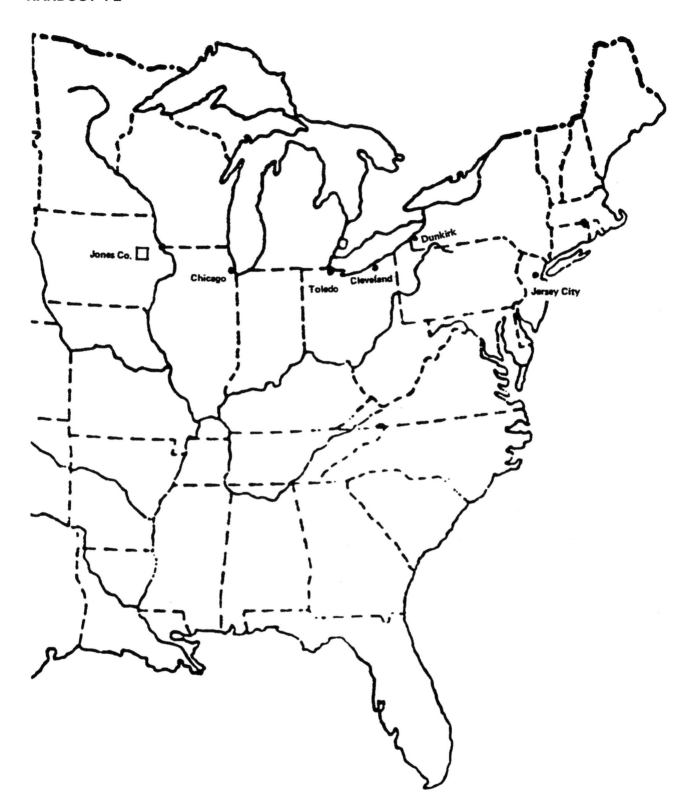

Directions. Mark the route of the Fairchild travelers, color-coding the route according to the means of transportation.

Activity 4-3: PRAIRIE FIRES

Skills. Collecting information from primary source materials

Materials. Kenyon letter (in text)

Procedure

1. Introduce the letter by reviewing some of the hardships and dangers encountered by pioneer settlers on the prairie.
2. Read and discuss the Kenyon letter with the students.
3. Using the information in the text and the letter, have students compose a pamphlet for new settlers on the prairie, warning them of the dangers of prairie fires and instructing them on how to protect themselves from an approaching fire. Encourage students to use quotes of eyewitnesses (John Kenyon) and use illustrations in the pamphlet.

Activity 4-4: BUYING LAND IN FRONTIER IOWA

Skills. Collecting information from primary source materials and reading maps

Materials. Township diagram (in text), President Tyler's Proclamation (in text), handout 4-4 *(Iowa Territory 1842* map)

Procedure

1. Open the class by rereading the material in the chapter on surveying and purchasing land. Discuss the township system, identifying and defining the following terms:

baseline	range
county	section
5th principal meridian	township
proclamation	

2. Discuss the proclamation of President Tyler and the township and section diagrams.
3. Distribute copies of handout 4-4. Have students locate and shade the townships identified in President Tyler's proclamation.

Name _____

Directions. Shade the townships and quarter sections (not lots) listed in President Tyler's proclamation of September 27, 1842. You may want to refer to the township diagram.

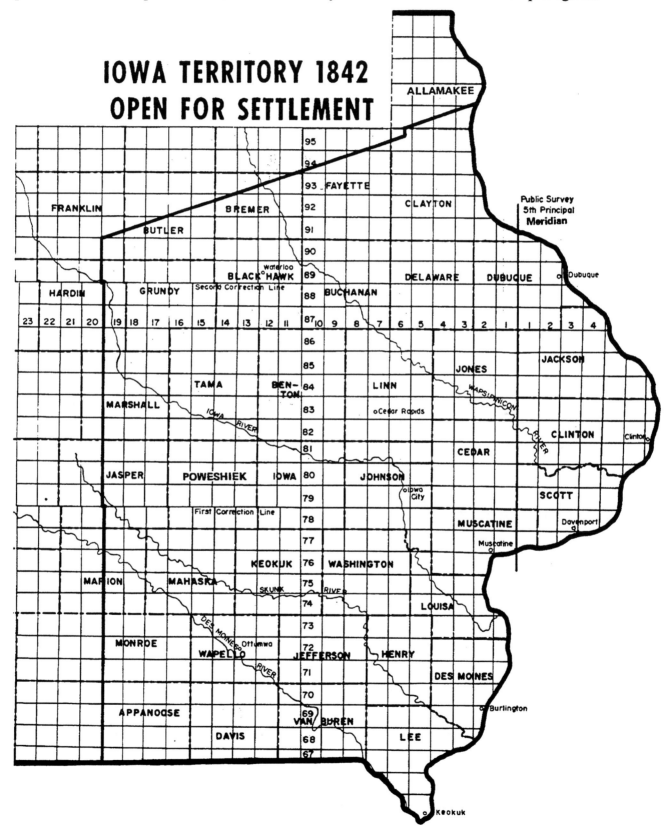

5 Pioneer Life on the Prairie

CONTENT OBJECTIVES

Following the completion of the readings and activities for this chapter, students will have acquired the following understandings:

a. Pioneers raised or made most of the items they needed for daily life.
b. Pioneer families developed a sense of social community and interdependence by sharing work and social events.

VOCABULARY TO KNOW

loom   sod house

poultice   spinning wheel

puncheon flooring   straw pallet

root cellar

FOR FURTHER STUDY

A visit to Living History Farms near Des Moines will provide firsthand observation of pioneer life on the prairie. The 1850 farm and the 1900 farm both provide a window into the lives of pioneer settlers.

REFERENCES

Birch, Brian P. "Possessed of a Restless Spirit: A Young Girl's Memories of the Southern Iowa Frontier." *The Palimpsest* 66, no. 5 (September/October 1985). Iowa City: State Historical Society of Iowa.

Bonney, Margaret, ed. "Early Agriculture." *The Goldfinch* 2, no. 3 (February 1981). Iowa City: State Historical Society of Iowa.

Connolly, Loris, and Agatha Huepenbecker. "Home Weaving in Southeast Iowa, 1833-1870." *The Annals of Iowa* 48, nos. 1, 2 (Summer/Fall 1985). Iowa City: State Historical Society of Iowa.

DeQuille, Dan. "Trailing a Lost Child." *The Palimpsest* 69, no. 3 (Fall 1988). Iowa City: State Historical Society of Iowa.

1870 Iowa State Almanac. Explorations in Iowa History Project. Cedar Falls: Malcolm Price Laboratory School, University of Northern Iowa.

Emily Hawley Gillespie Diaries, Sarah Huftalen Collection, Manuscript Collection. Iowa City: State Historical Society of Iowa.

Goranson, Rita. "Sod Dwellings in Iowa." *The Palimpsest* 65, no. 4 (July-August 1984). Iowa City: State Historical Society of Iowa.

Preston, Julia Antoinette Losee. "Washtub Over the Sun." *The Palimpsest* 68, no. 1 (Spring 1987). Iowa City: State Historical Society of Iowa.

Riley, Glenda. *Frontierswomen*. Ames: Iowa State University Press, 1981.

_____. "Prairie Partnerships." *The Palimpsest* 69, no. 2 (Summer 1988). Iowa City: State Historical Society of Iowa.

Throne, Mildred. "'Book Farming' in Iowa, 1840-1870." In *Patterns and Perspectives in Iowa History*, Dorothy Schwieder, ed. Ames: Iowa State University Press, 1973.

Activity 5-1: COMPARING PIONEER HOMES

Skills. Reading maps and creating charts from given data or information

Materials. Map of five frontiers of the Iowa pioneers, *1870 Iowa State Almanac* account of pioneer building (in text), student copies of handout 5-1

Procedure

1. Find map of frontiers of settlement in Iowa (in text). Discuss the progressive settlement of Iowa between 1840 and 1870. Discuss the relationship between the type of land and the type of homes built in the frontier period. Trees were plentiful in southeast Iowa, and thus log cabins were common. Trees were less prevalent in northwest Iowa, thus sod homes were more common.

2. Allow time for students to read the instructions for making each type of house. Distribute copies of handout 5-1. Have students work with partners to complete the chart.

Name _____

COMPARING LOG CABINS AND SOD HOUSES

	Sod Houses	Log Cabins
Materials needed		
Advantages		
Disadvantages		
Typical location in Iowa		

Directions. Using the information in the text, complete this chart.

Activity 5-2: THE CROWDED CABIN

Skills. Collecting information from secondary source material

Materials. Large sheets of wrapping paper, tape or string for partitioning the room

Procedure

1. Prior to class, partition off a sixteen-by-eighteen-foot section of the classroom using tape or string. Have the students sit down inside the space, identifying the area as being the size of a typical cabin.
2. Read and discuss the section of the text chapter titled, "Building Homes on the Prairie" while sitting together in the "cabin."
3. Using the large sheets of wrapping paper, have students make the various items found in the cabin by placing appropriately sized pieces of paper on the floor as place holders. Designate locations for doors and windows.
4. Discuss the crowded conditions often found inside a cabin and the implications this had for the lives of the pioneers.

6 Rivers, Trails, and Train Tracks

TRANSPORTATION IN THE 1800s

CONTENT OBJECTIVES

Following the completion of the readings and activities for this chapter, students will have acquired the following understandings:

a. Transportation was very important for Iowa's early pioneers. Not only was it important for people coming to Iowa, but after arriving, people relied on transportation for their livelihoods.
b. The major means of commercial transportation—steamboat, stagecoach, and railroad—developed significantly during the 19th century.
c. Each of these means of transportation had positive and negative aspects, and each helped Iowa develop economically.
d. The railroad was the most important form of transportation for 19th-century Iowa. It was faster and more dependable than any other form of transportation. It greatly assisted new settlers coming to the state and also aided in the development of new industry.

VOCABULARY TO KNOW

cargo, freight	luxurious
cholera	merchandise
corporation	Old Northwest
crossroads	platting
deck passage	railroad survey, surveyor
dehydration	Robert Fulton's Clermont
epidemics	transportation

FOR FURTHER STUDY

1. Have students explore how Iowa's transportation systems today compare to transportation in pioneer Iowa.

2. Encourage students to explore reasons why other forms of transportation replaced the railroad as the most important form of travel.

3. Between 1850 and 1930 steam locomotives averaged 65 miles per hour; today jet airplanes reach speeds in excess of 600 miles per hour. Ask students to contemplate how this change in travel time affects Iowa's economy. They may want to develop a list of consequences of this decrease in travel time.

4. Have students write letters of inquiry to Chambers of Commerce in several of Iowa's river towns (such as Dubuque or Sioux City) requesting information on how the rivers affect their economy today. Students may also want to study the history of one or more of these cities. This would require extending the time allotted to this topic.

REFERENCES

Boeck, George A. "A Decade of Transportation Fever in Burlington, Iowa, 1845–1855." In *Patterns and Perspectives in Iowa History*, Dorothy Schwieder, ed. Ames: Iowa State University Press, 1973.

Bonney, Margaret, ed. "Railroads...." *The Goldfinch* 5, no. 2 (November 1983). Iowa City: State Historical Society of Iowa.

Deiss, Ron W. "'Shortening the River:' Henry Bosse's Images of the Changing Mississippi." *The Palimpsest* 78, no. 3 (Fall 1997). Iowa City: State Historical Society of Iowa.

Larson, Arthur Q. "Railroaders and Newspapers; The Dubuque Controversy of 1867." *The Annals of Iowa* 48, nos. 3, 4 (Winter/Summer 1986). Iowa City: State Historical Society of Iowa.

Larson, Lawrence H. "Urban Iowa One Hundred Years Ago." *The Annals of Iowa* 49, no. 6 (Fall 1988). Iowa City: State Historical Society of Iowa.

MacGregor, Greg. "Photographing the Mormon Trail Across the West." *The Palimpsest* 78, no. 2 (Summer 1997). Iowa City: State Historical Society of Iowa.

Parker, Leonard F. "Professor Parker before and in Early Grinnell." *Proceedings of the Old Settlers' Association of Grinnell, Iowa*, 1896-1901. L. F. Parker Collection, Section 2, 14-15. Iowa City: State Historical Society of Iowa.

Schwieder, Dorothy. "Town Life in the Middle Land." In *Iowa: The Middle Land*. Iowa State University Press, 1996. Chapter 2, Section 9.

Schwieder, Dorothy. "Urban Life in the Hawkeye State." In *Iowa: The Middle Land*. Iowa State University Press, 1996. Chapter 2.

Swaim, Ginalie, ed. "Rivers in Iowa." *The Goldfinch* 6, no.4 (April 1985). Iowa City: State Historical Society of Iowa.

William Buxton Diary, 1853-1860. Ruth B. Sayre Collection. Iowa City: State Historical Society of Iowa. National Railway Publication Company, 424 West 33rd Street, New York NY 10001.

Williams-Searle, John. "Counting Risk: Disability, Masculinity, and Liability on Iowa's Railroads, 1868-1950." *The Annals of Iowa* 58, no. 1 (Winter 1999). State Historical Society of Iowa.

Activity 6-1: THE GREAT BURLINGTON ROUTE

Skills. Reading and interpreting graphic information

Materials. Railroad advertisements in text, student handout 6-1

Procedure

1. Introduce the lesson by asking students to identify ways in which commercial transportation companies today publicize their services. Discuss various means of advertising used by these companies.

2. Distribute copies of handout 6-1. Provide time for students to complete the questions.

3. Conclude the lesson by sharing observations about railroad travel in the 19th century and comparing methods of travel then with today.

Directions. The two advertisements in the text were taken from a travel guide for Iowans traveling on the railroad. After looking closely at these advertisements, answer the following questions.

1. Use a dictionary to find what the following terms mean.

parlor _____

patent _____

porter _____

destination _____

parcel _____

chandeliers _____

2. What is the name of the railroad company for which this ad was made? _____

_____

3. What special features did these railroad cars have? _____

_____

_____

4. How does the railroad help protect passengers' baggage? _____

_____

5. In your own words, describe the inside of a parlor car _____

_____

_____

_____

Activity 6-2: COMPARING EARLY IOWA TRANPORTATION

Skills. Skimming written material for specific information

Materials. Student copies of handout 6-2

Procedure

1. Begin the lesson by reviewing pioneer Iowa's major means of commercial travel (steamboat, railroad, and stagecoach). Discuss the advantages and disadvantages of each.

2. Distribute copies of handout 6-2. Provide time for students to complete the chart using their textbooks and other resource materials.

3. Conclude the lesson by comparing the various characteristics of each means of travel.

Name _____

COMPARING EARLY IOWA TRANSPORTATION

	Steamboat	Stagecoach	Railroad
Advantages			
Disadvantages			
Parts of Iowa where used			
Cargo that could be carried			
Industries / businesses helped by this transportation			

Directions. Using your textbook and other resource material, complete this chart.

Activity 6-3: TRAVELING WITH WILLIAM BUXTON

Skills. Reading primary source materials

Materials. Journal of William Buxton (in text), student copies of handouts 6-3a, 6-3b, 6-3c, 6-3d, 6-3e

Procedure

1. Introduce the lesson by providing background information on William Buxton. The diary reprinted in the text is a selection from a larger journal kept between 1853 and 1860.

BIOGRAPHICAL SKETCH

William Buxton, a native of Derbyshire, England, migrated to the United States in 1851 at the age of twenty-one. He located in Carlisle, Iowa, and acquired a quarter section of land (160 acres). Two years later, his uncle in England died, leaving him $2,000 in cash. He returned to England to claim his inheritance. On his trip back to the United States, he kept a daily account of his travel experiences. This journal is his record.

Buxton later married Betsy Bramhall. She had moved to Warren County, Iowa, with her parents. The Buxtons had five children, one son and four daughters. For seventeen years, they lived in a log cabin before building a frame house.

Buxton farmed outside of Carlisle for forty years. In 1892 he moved to Indianola, where he assumed management of the Warren County State Bank. He added to his farmland, owning 1400 acres at the time of his death. Simpson College received support from Buxton; he gave it large sums of money and land. He died in Indianola in 1919 at the age of 89.

2. Briefly discuss what Iowa was like in 1853 to provide the setting for the journal. Divide the class into five groups and provide each group with one of the activity sheets. Allow time for the groups to complete the activities.

3. Discuss the responses by having a student from each group describe the activity of his/her group and summarize the group's conclusions for the class.

4. Conclude this lesson by having students discuss which form of transportation was best for Buxton, substantiating their views using information from the journal.

Directions. Use the journal of William Buxton to answer these questions.

1. What age was Buxton when he made this trip? _____

2. For what reason did he make the trip? _____

    _____

3. What was the name of the ocean steamship on which Buxton took passage? _____

    _____

4. List the kinds of transportation used by Buxton on his trip. _____

    _____

5. Which river steamboats were used by Buxton? _____

    _____

6. From which English city did he begin his return trip to Iowa? _____

    _____

7. What was the date Buxton left England and when did he arrive in Carlisle, Iowa? How
   long did the journey take?

    _____

    _____

Names _____

FIGURING DISTANCE AND TIME FOR BUXTON'S TRAVELS

Entry in Journal	From	To	Type of Transportation	Number of Miles	Time	
					Days	Hours
Fri. Nov. 25	Liverpool, England	Philadelphia, PA				
Tues. Nov. 29	Philadelphia, PA	Wheeling, VA				
Wed. Dec. 13	Cincinnati, OH	St. Louis, MO				
Mon. Dec. 19	St. Louis, MO	Keokuk, IA				
Thurs. Dec. 22	Keokuk, IA	Ft. Des Moines, IA				
Sun. Dec 25	Ft. Des Moines, IA	Carlisle, IA				

Directions: Complete the table by finding the number of miles between the pairs of cities and the time spent in traveling between each pair of cities.

LEISURE ACTIVITIES WHILE TRAVELING IN 1853

Leisure Activity	Reported by Buxton	Leisure Activity	Reported by Buxton
Concerts		Bridge	
Dances		Chess/Checkers	
Fireworks display		Croquet	
Games		Poker	
Reading		Shuffleboard	
Singing		Theater	

Directions. Check the leisure-time activities reported by William Buxton in his journal.

Name _____

COMPARING BUXTON'S TRAVEL EXPERIENCES

Experience	Kind of Experience: P or B
Seasickness	
Meals on the *City of Glasgow*	
Meals on the *Latrobe*	
Buffenden Island	
Louisville, Kentucky	
Supper at Oskaloosa, Iowa	
Entertainment on the *City of Glasgow*	
Near-collision at sea	

Directions. Complete the chart by using the letter P to describe a pleasant experience of Buxton's, the letter B to describe one of his bad travel experiences.

Name _____

WILLIAM BUXTON'S TRAVEL PROBLEMS

Directions. Place a check mark before the hazards reported by William Buxton in his journal.

_____ Seasickness

_____ Broken axle on stagecoach

_____ Possible collision with another vessel

_____ Steamboat stuck on sandbar

_____ River too low for steamboats

_____ Train derailed

_____ Charged fare twice for steamboat trip

_____ Poor quality food on steamboat

_____ Danger of ice in the river

_____ Cholera epidemic along Mississippi River

[Note: The uncut version of Buxton's journal may help answer some of the questions on the worksheets.]

1853

Nov. 7—Monday. Left Nottingham early, on my return voyage to the land of the West bidding adieu to the scene of many happy hours spent in the company of those who will ever retain a place in my best affections and thoughts. Went over to Disbury where I spent the night and accompanied by Mrs. Hobbs and Miss Lack returned to Manchester where after making several bargains I received the last well wishes of the many friends I have learned to value as well as many other things with which old England abounds above all other lands.

Nov. 8—Tuesday. Tuesday arrived in Liverpool and took passage in the screw steamship "City of Glasgow" for Philadelphia, Captain Whylie.

Nov. 9—Wednesday. Went on board the steamer then lying in the river which being all tight started on her trip about half past one o'clock p.m. favored by the tide and clear sky.

Nov. 10—Thursday. Steaming down channel with head wind run 160 mls to 12 p.m.

Nov. 11—Friday. Irish coast in view head wind and clear sky pretty rough sea nearly all sick, myself among [the] lot dreadfully sick and good for nothing vowed never to cross again except on my return. Course N.W. run 192.

Nov. 12—Saturday. Feeling rather curious but after eating a good dinner was as fresh and content as ever. Course West run 188. Wednesday midnight we had a most hair-breath escape of being run down by a large [vessel] in full sail which came so close as to carry away part of our rigging; a few feet nearer we should have met with certain destruction to many if not all of us, but as it is we are proceeding prosperously on the voyage and I hope thankful for our safety.

Nov. 13—Sunday. Fine and pleasant service at 1/2 past ten conducted by the Captain according to the Church of Scotland. Course WNW run 210.

Nov. 15—Tuesday. Fine, getting quite jolly and friendly now on board spending the day in reading and games, the evenings in concerts. Course N.W. Run 199.

Nov. 16—Wednesday. with strong breeze which increased during the day and the sea running pretty high knocking us about in all directions, and causing us no little inconvenience and a good many cases of sickness appeared again. Run 100 mls.

Nov. 17—Thursday. All quiet again today very glad to see it so and now begin to relish the meals which are served up as follows. breakfast at 8 & 9 dinner 1 & 3 supper 6 & 7 o'clock provided on a very liberal scale. C. West run 146 mls.

Nov. 18—Friday. Past a very rough night, the sea now running what is term'd mountains high, the finest I have ever seen, hope it may not last long, too cold to be on deck. the ship Sam Barker to Liverpool running before the wind with main & top sails a beautiful sight as seen from our ship. Run 190 mls. This was the day fixed for the grand concert and dress ball on quarter deck (weather permitting) but that not being the case it is deferred sine die to our great disappointment. At dinner there was a perfect commotion among the crockery, ducks fowls beef & soup all alive occasionally some unfortunate dish would come sliding majestically on to the floor, and requiring some effort to keep one's seat at the table.

Nov. 19—Saturday. Fine & Pleasant but head wind C.N.W. run 104 mls. Saw the first porpoises this voyage

Nov. 20—Sunday. Dry and cold moderate & favorable wind as we are passed at 8 p.m. a mail steamer which left N. Fork last Wednesday signals were given & returned rockets were first thrown up from our ship and answered by the same number from the other. The night was clear and the effect of the scene was very startling and pleasing. Run 200 mls.

Nov. 21—Monday. Fine & pleasant & fair wind 12 p.m. run 209 mls. This evening we had our celebrated concert commencing at 7 1/2 o'clock embracing most of the celebrated pieces of (Music) both vocal and instrumental piano concertina and accordian. The Mid amused us with some very original singing, the old Batchelor. What are little girls made of & Father Stevens made an attempt but was sadly deficient in voice. Molly (Coover) was very amusing. After the concert the company adjourned to the quarter deck to witness the fireworks which were very imposing. Then came the dance, concluding with supper in saloon. Appropriate songs and toasts, altogether the evening was spent very pleasantly. The captain did everything to entertain the company and fully deserved the good name he has [won] already.

Nov. 22—Tuesday. Fine and steady winds run 233 mls.

Nov. 23—Wednesday. 12 p.m. Last night we had the first theatrical performance on board the comic farce of Box & Box & Mrs. Bouncer the lodging housekeeper, Messrs Mienty-Gibbons & Kendall were the performers the whole scene was very laughable and went off with great eclat. There was a concert going on at the same time in the forward cabin. We have had beautiful weather the last few days, time passed very pleasantly and not at all monotonous as is generally the case. Wednesday run 200 mls.

Nov. 24—Thursday. Still very calm & fine too vessels astern expect to be in Philadelphia by Saturday. Run 213 steam only.

Nov. 25—Friday. Last night the wind got up blowing strong, the sea changing in a few hours from a perfect calm to the opposite extreme but settled down considerably this morning. passed a beautiful clipper built ship hoisted American colors. Looking out for pilot boat. Run 233 mls. Course W .S. W .1/2 W. about 2 o'clock today we took on the pilot and in a few hours more the land appeared ahead Cape May on our right. The shore all along is low and sandy. Philadelphia lies about 100 miles up the Delaware a fine broad stream with a fine country on both sides. We anchored in the river at night and came along side the pier about 1 o'clock Saturday making a passage of seventeen days 3275 miles.

Nov. 26—Saturday. Myself and four others took up our quarters at Bloodwood corner of Walnut St. Took a [tour] through the City, which is one of the finest in The States. Chestnut St. the principal thoroughfare contained some splendid buildings. Hotels and besides being the great promenade for the fashionable. I think the ladies of Philadelphia surpass anything I ever saw in any other city for beauty and dress.

Nov. 27—Sunday. Attended St. Stephens Episcopal Church the sermon more political than religious thorough Whig. Left with a friend for New York by rail.

Nov. 28—Monday. Arranging business matters, went to the Exhibition which quite met my anticipation there were a great many things worthy of attention and was only sorry I had not more time to examine its contents. The [statuary] was the most attractive and next the agricultural department returned to Philadelphia at night (per) Camden and Amboy.

Nov. 29—Tuesday. Took ticket for Cincinnati via Baltimore and Ohio rail to Wheeling then a boat on the river. Left Phil. at 2 p.m. arriving at Wheeling 2 1/2 p.m. Wednesday 490 miles. The railroad runs direct over the Alegany mountains almost impassable, winding round the hills and overlooking some precipices truly fearful and certain death in case of any mishap one journey is quite sufficient to satisfy any traveller especially when he knows that the works are anything but substantial.

Nov. 30—Wednesday. Left Wheeling at 4 p.m. by the Latrobe, should be in Cincinnati early on Friday but am afraid I shall be disappointed. The river being low the regular packets run there are twice the number of passengers on board there ought to be one half without berths a western traveller has plenty of exercise for a good stock of patience as well as a little *smartness.*

Dec. 1—Thursday. Going along at a snail gallop. The banks all along are high and steep dotted over with many little towns. Just had dinner, a few scraps of all sorts, goes bad after having such good fare so long on board the "City of Glasgow."

Dec. 2—Friday. Moving slowly down the river expecting every minute to come to a stand, several other boats being fast and stopping the navigation. In the evening most of the passengers were prevailed upon to go ashore in order to lighten a little and a good part of the freight put ashore but notwithstanding every endeavor the boat stuck fast alongside four others near Buffenden Island. We passengers were now in a fix having no means of getting aboard again until a yawl was got taking four passengers at a time with considerable danger.

Dec. 3—Saturday. Still fast and with every prospect of a famine on board. hearing of a boat, being below, for Cincinnati we all left the "Latrobe" sending our baggage and the ladies down in canoes. The gents walked down to the boat. The "Crystal Palace" a splendid boat, good fare, which they took care to get paid for many of the passengers having to pay a second full fare however I was glad to get off on any terms.

Dec. 4—Sunday. Arrived late in evening at Cincinnati.

Dec. 5—Monday. Took boat for Lawrenceburg 20 mls where I had to remain until morning for the cars to Flatrock.

Dec. 6—Tuesday. Landed at Ben's just in time for a good dinner and found them all well things improving fast. Looking round and visiting the rest of the week.

Dec. 11—Sunday. Went to meeting in the new Court House heard a pretty good sermon in the evening took tea at the Avery's, one of the nicest families at Flatrock.

Dec. 12—Monday. Took the cars for Lawrenceburg & boat to Cincinnati went to see the pork slaughter yards which is carried on here on a large scale, a thousand hogs being a day's work for one set of hands to kill & pack, but rather roughly done.

Dec. 13—Tuesday. Got on the Ben Franklin for Louisville and St. Louis, which left at 12 p.m. reaching Louisville in twelve hours 15 mls.

Dec. 14—Wednesday. Took the bus down to Portland since round the falls the water being too low to allow the boats to pass over, and got aboard the "Fashion" for St. Louis 700 mls from Cincinnati entered the Mississippi Friday noon. Took on a lot of Californians at Cairo bound home, some with a good "pile" others with disappointed hopes only.

Dec. 18—Sunday. Arrived early this morning at St. Louis winter having set in hard pretty near closed navigation on the upper river however determined to risk a day or two longer in town taking up quarters at the City Hotel until Monday. Attended service in morning at the Episcopal Church. Here I met with several of my ship mates and an English gentleman, Rutherford, who was well acquainted with Derbyshire.

Dec. 19—Monday. Got my drafts exchanged after a good deal of trouble. Then started off at 6 p.m. for Keokuk 215 mls on the "Dubuque", probably the last boat to ascend the Mississippi this season—it being both difficult & dangerous on account of the ice which is fast choking up the river and very thick in some places. The upper Mississippi is far more interesting than the lower (so far as I have been) beautifully studded with islands and fine high bluffs. The water above the Missouri is perfectly clear and transparent.

Dec. 20—Tuesday. The river rather more open this morning but making very slow progress. Passed some flourishing towns on the Miss. side.

Dec. 21—Wednesday. Morning arrived safe at Keokuk the end of my river travelling and very glad of it. In time of high water it is very pleasant but miserable at low stages. Most of the captains & inferior officers are generally nothing but a lot of sharpers!

Dec. 22—Thursday. Had to lie over until Thursday morning for the stage which left at 4 a.m. for Fort D'Moines 180 mls.

Dec. 24—Saturday. The roads being good we got on pretty fast, travelling it in three days, first night at Fairfield, 2nd, Oskaloosa where we just came in right for a bear meat supper and ball the first was excellent, the latter very commonplace. Arrived at the Fort about seven Saturday evening, pretty well tired of the stage.

Dec. 25—Sunday. Xmas day walked over to Carlisle 12 mls, which is to be my future home, where I found all things about as when I left after an absence of about nine months during which time I had traveled 12000 miles without any misfortune.

FROM: William Buxton Diary, 1853-1860. Ruth B. Sayre Collection. Iowa City: State Historical Society of Iowa.

7   A Nation Divided

CONTENT OBJECTIVES

Following the completion of the readings and activities for this chapter, students will have acquired the following understandings:

a. Iowa was created as a free state according to the Missouri Compromise, and most Iowans were glad slavery was prohibited in Iowa.
b. Iowans helped slaves escape to freedom by working on the underground railroad.
c. Although no Civil War battles were fought in Iowa, many Iowans were directly involved in the Civil War.
d. Numerous regiments of Iowa soldiers were sent to battle, while many Iowa women ran the farms and businesses. Women also helped with the war effort by sending supplies to soldiers far from home.
e. Some Iowans, known as Copperheads, were actively opposed to the Civil War.

VOCABULARY TO KNOW

Civil War	quota
Confederate States	racial segregation
Copperhead	Republican party
Democratic party	slavery
diet kitchen	the South, the North
mustered out	underground railroad
orphans' homes	volunteer

PEOPLE TO IDENTIFY

Cyrus Carpenter   Abraham Lincoln

Jefferson Davis   Dennis Mahony

Grenville Dodge   General William T. Sherman

General Ulysses S. Grant   Reverend John Todd

George Wallace Jones   Annie Wittenmyer

FOR FURTHER STUDY

1. The State Capitol in Des Moines has on display an interesting collection of Civil War flags and uniforms. A visit to the statehouse to view these displays and the other interesting sights would lend much interest to a unit on Iowa in the Civil War.

2. Encourage students to visit the Civil War Days at Hopkinton, Iowa. Located on and near the Lenox College site in Hopkinton, events include a Civil War encampment, skirmish reenactments, and authentic Civil War band music. This event is usually held in early June.

REFERENCES

Danbom, David B. " 'Dear Companion': Civil War Letters of a Story County Farmer." *The Annals of Iowa* 47, no. 6 (Fall 1984). Iowa City: State Historical Society of Iowa.

Johnson, Russell L. " 'A Debt Justly Due:' The Relief of Civil War Soldiers and Their Families in Dubuque." *The Annals of Iowa* 55, no. 3 (Summer 1996). State Historical Society of Iowa.

Kuecker, Susan. "Reverberations of the War: Cedar Rapids in 1865." *Iowa Heritage Journal* 80, no. 3 (Fall 1999). State Historical Society of Iowa.

Lucas, Thomas A. " 'Men Were Too Fiery for Much Talk:' The Grinnell Anti-Abolitionism Riot of 1860." *The Palimpsest* 68, no. 1 (Spring 1987). State Historical Society of Iowa.

Lyftogt, Kenneth L. *From Blue Mills to Columbia: Cedar Falls and the Civil War*. Ames: Iowa State University Press, 1993.

Nelson, Julie E., and Alan M. Schroder. "Iowa and the Civil War: A Military Review." *The Palimpsest* 63, no. 4 (July / August 1982). Iowa City: State Historical Society of Iowa.

Leonard F. Parker. "Professor Parker before and in Early Grinnell." *Proceedings of the Old Settlers' Association of Grinnell, Iowa, 1896-1901.* 14-15. L. F. Parker Collection, Section 2. Iowa City: State Historical Society of Iowa.

Peterson, Richard W. "Tell the Boys I Die Happy." *The Palimpsest* 66, no.6 (November/December 1985). Iowa City: State Historical Society of Iowa.

Posten, Margaret L. *This is the Place-Iowa.* Ames: Iowa State University Press, 1970.

Sage, Leland L. *A History of Iowa* (Iowa Heritage Collection). Ames: Iowa State University Press, 1987. Chapter 9, "The Civil War 1861-1865."

Schwieder, Dorothy. "Iowans and the Civil War Era." In *Iowa: The Middle Land.*" Iowa State University Press, 1996. Chapter 1.

Vollertsen, Edward W. " 'A Pretty Hard Business:' The Civil War Diary of Phillip H. Goode." *The Palimpsest* 72, no. 2 (Summer 1991). State Historical Society of Iowa.

Wall, Joseph F. "We Fight for the Land." In *Iowa: A Bicentennial History.* New York: W. W. Norton, 1978. Chapter 6.

Activity 7-1: BLACKS AND PUBLIC SCHOOLING

Skills. Reading primary source material

Materials. Parker letter in text, student copies of handout 7-1

Procedure

1. Introduce the lesson by discussing the fact that although most Iowans were against slavery they still did not want blacks to live in Iowa. Iowans were not ready to accept blacks into society.

2. Read the Parker letter together as a class.

CONCLUSION TO THE GRINNELL RIOT

[Many years later, Leonard Parker recalled the outcome.]

"Discretion ... proved the better part of valor. The boys [blacks] were persuaded not to insist on their rights at that time. Grinnell's first and only embryo mob dissolved without a bloody termination. The term closed at once—a few days before the regular time—the boys engaged in summer work; the Civil War broke out. That solved the negro question for Grinnell and for many a place besides."

3. Use the following analysis questions to discuss the selection:

    1. Was Sarah Parker a black person or white?
    2. What was the topic of the school meeting on Monday night?
    3. What caused one man to shout, "They shall never enter those doors unless over my dead body?"
    4. Was there physical violence at Monday night's meeting?
    5. What did Sarah's husband do for a living?
    6. Were the two black students sincere about wanting to go to school? How do you know?
    7. According to the letter, what did Sarah Parker think would happen to church congregations following the riot? How might the conflict among the church members carry over to the business and social life of the town?
    8. According to Leonard F. Parker, what solved the school integration problem for Grinnell?

4. Distribute copies of handout 7-1. Provide students time to write a newspaper account of the events described in the letter of Sarah Parker. After sharing the students' written newspaper accounts, discuss and contrast the racial perceptions of the 1860s with today's perceptions.

Name _____

Grinnell Daily News

MARCH   1860

_____   _____

_____   _____

_____   _____

_____   _____

_____   _____

_____   _____

_____   _____

_____   _____

_____   _____

_____   _____

_____   _____

_____   _____

_____   _____

_____   _____

_____   _____

PRIMARY SOURCE MATERIAL: Sarah Parker's Account of the Grinnell Riot (unabridged)

Grinnell, March 10, 1860

My Dear Mother,

Your letter, commenced on my birthday, is just received. I had concluded that you were sick, when yesterday a letter from Aunt R. came to tell me you were.

I have long been trying to write, but we have had a very interesting series of meetings, and when they closed, my eyes became sore so that I could not use them much, and am now just able to write. ...

If my eyes were well and I had plenty of time and room, I would give you particulars of, what think you!—THE FIRST MOB IN GRINNELL!

Do not be astonished; it has been and is gone, but its effects can never be effaced from our community. You know, mother, that when the "Sons of God came to present themselves before the Lord—Satan came also among them." So it has been here.

I wrote to you Saturday evening Sunday those whom I mentioned were received into the church. Monday evening was a school meeting. To prepare you for what follows, I must relate (or write) a few facts. In the midst of our revival a Quaker brought for our safe keeping, four black men, whom the Tabor people helped to rescue from kidnappers. They were received, and offered work, as two of them wished to go back after their wives and children. They were anxious to learn and asked to go to school. Their employers consented to their going until the spring work came on. They went, but it offended many. The question—"Shall colored pupils be received in our schools?" was put to vote at the school meeting, and the ayes carried it by a small majority. One man arose in a frenzy of passion, exclaiming, "They shall never enter those doors unless over my dead body." Another says—"I go with you."—and still others said the same, telling the antislavery men they must come prepared to defend them if they send the negroes on. The proceedings of the meeting on the proslavery side were beyond belief. We who were graduates of Oberlin received torrents of abuse, ladies and all. ... Mrs. Augusta Bixby, the Squire's wife received her portion with us, because she is a decided antislavery and lets it be known. Mr. Cooper was called a liar to his face—he only replied "Very well." Mr. Parker silenced their slanders of Oberlin by giving them the facts. It was feared the meeting would not end without fighting—but it did.

Tuesday morning, between eight and nine, the mob came on to the school house, led by two of the most desperate men in town. The two negroes saw the proceedings and it roused their savage wrath. They armed themselves and came on, saying that if they must suffer so to gain their freedom, and have all these indignities heaped upon them after they had gained it, they might as well die at once. As the Blacks approached, the leaders of the mob went to the schoolhouse steps with clubs, and it is supposed, concealed weapons. By much persuasion, the negroes were prevented from attempting to meet them, but it was their preference to fight their way through. They would probably have killed their leaders. Then the mob called on the officers to disarm them, but they would not, for their lives had been threatened and they would not deprive them of the means of defense. Riot ran wild in our streets until noon, then a short calm ensued. Meetings for counsel were held on both sides—secret meetings by the mob, in which Mr. Parker and the negroes were the objects on which to vent their wrath.

Wednesday forenoon was as exciting as the day before. Desperate deeds were meditated—men maddened with hate and rage ran through the streets with insulting words ever on their lips. When I bade my husband good morning, I did not know but he would be the first victim of the fury. For he told the mob the day before that if they attempted to touch one of the pupils under his care, he should defend him. But we all live—though knives were whetted for hand to hand encounters, guns loaded and pistols made ready.

God restrains wrath when his purpose is accomplished. The town is not settled yet. We know not what to do. It will probably divide the church for several of the members were in the mob. The school, closed on account of the trouble, is to commence in three weeks.

FROM: L. F. Parker Collection, Section 2. Iowa City: State Historical Society of Iowa.

Activity 7-2: WOMEN IN THE CIVIL WAR

Skills. Writing reports

Materials. Reference books on Iowa history

Procedure

1. Begin the lesson by reminding students that both men and women in Iowa made major contributions to the war effort.

2. Have students identify various contributions which women provided. The following are possible responses:

> Maintained parenting responsibilities while men were away
> Ran businesses and farms
> Provided goods for soldiers
> Established relief societies to aid both soldiers and families.

3. Have students research and write reports on Annie Wittenmyer and Grenville Dodge. Compare and contrast the contributions these leaders made to the war effort. See the reference list for resources that provide information on these important Iowans.

Activity 7-3: CIVIL WAR MAP

Skills. Reading for sequence

Materials. Reference materials on Civil War, student copies of handout 7-3

Procedure

1. Review the material in the chapter on the movements of the Second Iowa Infantry Regiment.

2. Distribute copies of handout 7-3.

3. Group the students in pairs. Using reference materials in the room and the material from the chapter, have students trace the movements of the Second Iowa Infantry Regiment as recounted in the textbook.

4. In addition, have student color-code the maps, identifying slave and free states, territories, and unorganized regions in the United States during the Civil War.

5. Display completed maps on a classroom bulletin board.

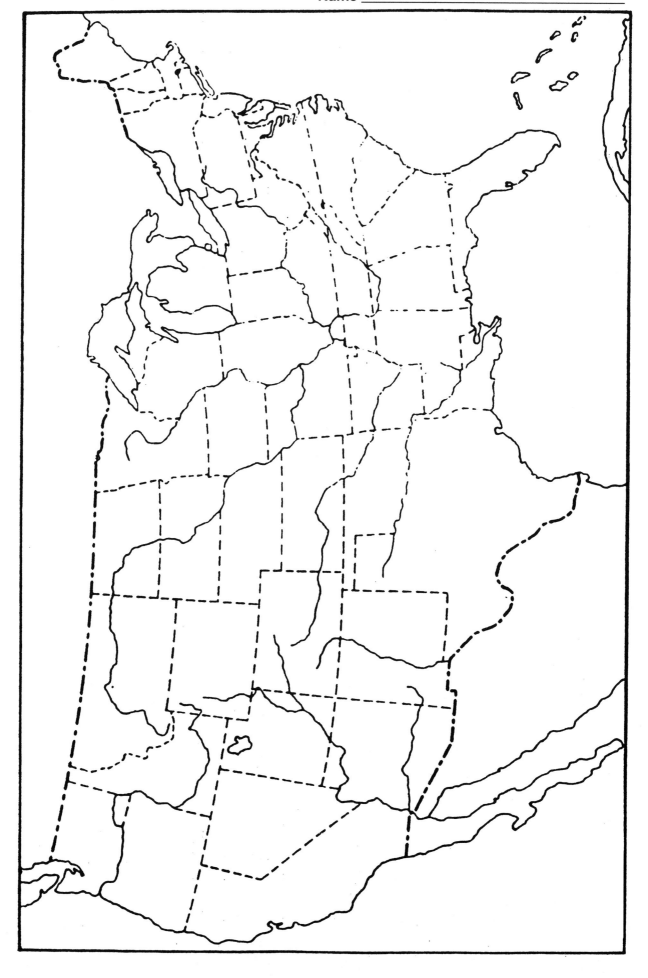

Activity 7-4: IOWA'S ROLE IN THE CIVIL WAR

Skills. Skimming for specific information

Materials. Transparency 7-4

Procedure

1. Begin the lesson by reviewing the fact that the Civil War was very costly to the nation, and particularly to the states where battles took place.
2. Project transparency 7-4. By skimming for information in the textbook, have students help complete the chart by contrasting how the Civil War affected Iowa compared to states in the South.

IOWA'S ROLE IN THE CIVIL WAR
(suggested responses)

What Iowans Contributed	Results of the Civil War for Iowans	Results of the Civil War for Southern States
Soldiers	Loss of life	Great loss of life
Women's support services	Economic slowdown	Great loss of property
Taxes	Hardship for many families	Economic disaster
Supplies		Slaves freed

IOWA'S ROLE IN THE CIVIL WAR

What Iowans Contributed	Results of the Civil War for Iowans	Results of the Civil War for Southern States
————————	————————	————————
————————	————————	————————
————————	————————	————————
————————	————————	————————
————————	————————	————————
————————	————————	————————
————————	————————	————————
————————	————————	————————
————————	————————	————————
————————	————————	————————
————————	————————	————————
————————	————————	————————

8   Settlers from Many Lands

CONTENT OBJECTIVES

Following the completion of the readings and activities for this chapter, students will have acquired the following understandings:

a. All Iowans have ancestors who immigrated to Iowa from other parts of the United States or the world (although American Indians came a few thousand years before the rest.)
b. People immigrated to Iowa for many reasons, including "push-pull factors" and events related to World War I.
c. Numerous ethnic settlements with unique customs and traditions were started in Iowa. Several festivals featuring the cultural traditions of these ethnic groups are held annually across the state.
d. Today Iowa continues to be a home for immigrants from all over the world, including newcomers from Bosnia, the Sudan, and additional immigrants from Mexico.

VOCABULARY TO KNOW

census	literacy
conscription	push-pull factors
discrimination	refugees
ethnic	rosemaling
Europe	settlement
freedom	Turner Society
generation	utopia
immigrant	

FOR FURTHER STUDY

1. Interview recent immigrants to your community. Ask them to share how they chose Iowa as their home.

2. Using the yellow pages of the local phone book, have students identify businesses and institutions which reflect a particular ethnic group and make contributions to the community.

3. Have students gather information on the various ethnic festivals held throughout the state. Using a classroom map, mark the location of each festival and display significant background information, such as ethnic group origin, date, etc. For information contact the Iowa Department of Economic Development.

REFERENCES

Beltman, Brian W. "Ethnic Persistence and Charge: The Experience of a Dutch-American Family in Rural Iowa." *The Annals of Iowa* 52, no. 1 (Winter 1993). Iowa City: State Historical Society of Iowa.

Birch, Brian P. "The Editor and the English: George Sheppard and English Immigration to Clinton County." *The Annals of Iowa* 47, no.8 (Spring 1985). Iowa City: State Historical Society of Iowa.

Bonney, Margaret, ed. "Immigrants," *The Goldfinch* 3, no.2 (November 1981). Iowa City: State Historical Society of Iowa.

Cooper, Arnie. "A Stony Road: Black Education in Iowa, 1838-1860." *The Annals of Iowa* 48, nos. 3, 4 (Winter/Spring 1986). Iowa City: State Historical Society of Iowa.

Graber, William B. "An Amish Mennonite Farmer Chooses Iowa." *The Palimpsest* 69, no. 4 (Winter 1988). Iowa City: State Historical Society of Iowa.

Kenyon, John B., and Sarah Kenyon Collection. Iowa City: State Historical Society of Iowa.

London, Minnie B. "As I Remember." Hubert L. Olin Papers. Des Moines, Iowa: State Historical Society of Iowa.

Otting, Loras C. "Gothic Splendor in Northeast Iowa." *The Palimpsest* 66, no.5 (September/October 1985). Iowa City: State Historical Society of Iowa.

Schwieder, Dorothy. "Cultural Diversity: Immigrants and African Americans in the Hawkeye State, 1833-80." In *Iowa: The Middle Land.*" Iowa State University Press, 1996. Chapter 1.

Schwieder, Dorothy. *Black Diamonds.* Ames: Iowa State University Press, 1983.

Swierenga, Robert P. "A Dutch Immigrant's View of Frontier Iowa." In *Patterns and Perspectives in Iowa History*, Dorothy Schwieder, ed. Ames: Iowa State University Press, 1973.

Thompson, Jerome. "Land and Personal Sovereignty." *The Palimpsest* 69, no. 2 (Summer 1988). Iowa City: State Historical Society of Iowa.

Activity 8-1: DESCRIBING IOWA TO A FRIEND

Skills. Summarizing and personalizing historical information

Materials. Writing paper, Letter of Sarah and John Kenyon

Procedure

1. Introduce the lesson by reading the Kenyon letter to students. Sarah Kenyon came to Iowa with her husband John, traveling from Rhode Island in 1856. She wrote many such letters back to her relatives in the East to let them know what it was like to live in pioneer Iowa.

2. Distribute writing paper to students. Ask them to write letters back home as if

they were recent immigrants to Iowa in 1856. Whether they select an eastern state or a European country as home, students should describe their lives on the frontier from the viewpoint of a pioneer settler.

3. Conclude the lesson by having students share their letters with the class. Letters might be illustrated with drawings or maps.

Letter of Sarah and John Kenyon
(Reproduced in its original form)

Plum Creek
Aug 29 (1856)

(Sarah Kenyon)

... Our goods have all arrived. The last that were sent came on the same time as our others. The stove hearth was broken into and Housing the slide pretty well smashed. We can have the hearth mended I think but the slide is past pancakes. everything else came safe and sound. ...

Our folks went after plums yesterday and I went a week ago. we travel in ox teams here over the prairies. It was the first time I had been in the woods since we came here. it was really refreshing to get in the shade and hear the birds sing. When I buy my farm I shall be near my timber ... .

Mr Parsons sold his farm a week ago for 27 hundred part prairie and part timber joining and is going farther west about two hundred miles. his wife feels very bad about it. I dont blame her. I have always looked at their place and thought it the prettiest place about here. there house stands near to the grove of timber. but any of the Westers are ready to sell anytime to make money. Mr Parsons paid six hundred for his two years ago so he thinks he will sell and go and make another good farm and sell again. I warrant all he has done to this one was to break and fence 20 or 30 acres. there was an old log hut on it that they have lived in since he came here without a window and so cold in Winter they have to go to bed to keep from freesing. that is what one of his boys told here. isnt it a shame a man worth between three and four thousand to live so but its the way of the world here.

We get along and do without things here that would be impossible in the East. I should dread for our neighbors to come and see us if they were not going to stay and settle. if so well and good for they would soon see the way of Western life ...

Wednesday forenoon I must try to steal a few minutes to write so as to get my letter finished to send to the office the first time Mail any one goes that way. it is not here as it was to Ashaway. you have to write and wait an opportunity to get it to the office. five miles over those prairies is quite a piece.

Tomorrow there will be ten dozen men here to thresh wheat so I shall get but previous little time to write then. Our freight bill was enormous on our goods but I dont see what we could have spared very well. we get along with what we brought. all that I have bought is half dozen cups & saucers. we have to snub it but that is what I knew we should have to do but as long as we have enough to eat I shall feel pretty well satisfied. We dont have nay dainties but we shall live just as long and perhaps be the healthier.

Molasses is eighty five cts per gallon sugar you can get 6, 8 and 9 pounds for a dollar. I did want to do up some plums but I cannot this year. great ones most as big as peaches.

green tea such as we get there for forty cts is one dollar. We shall have to go on credit for a year then if John has his health I hope we can do pretty well. He has got his cow most paid for. I feel very thinkful for that and (he) has bought two more heifers. I dont know how he will manage to pay for them but if he cant why he must sell them. it is not like buying Livestock clothing or any such thing for they will sell and keep gaining too. I really want to keep them through the winter if possible as he has got his hay cut and they would sell then for a great deal more than what he gave. He bought them to a sale on three months credit last month for eighteen dollars of the same man he bought his cow of ... .

a mink killed (Clara's) old white hen and part of the chickens so I had to take six of the chickens into the house ... Mrs. Robberts gave she and Bub a Shangai rooster and pullet. their names are Tom & Bet. I expect every night will be their last for the roost is not good for any thing and the owls minks and hawks are ready to help themselves the first opportunity. If they will keep off untill John can build a roost I will thank them very kindly ...

I begin to dread the Winter. they tell such cold stories about here. they said last Winter was awful by generally the Winters are very mild so much so that the ground dont freese untill about January but last Winter their floors would ice when they mopped and the tables when they washed dishes. Mr Barnard froze his great toe one night. it happened to get out of bed when he was asleep ... people as a general thing clothe the west with to much romance I take it. its not all gold that shines ...

[Note from John Kenyon on same letter]

... we have dug a well since we have been here and I finished stoneing it up yesterday. I have been a thrashing this week. we had 1,00. 15 (sic. 115) bushels wheat. they use thrashing machines here. it requires 8 horses and ten men to tend them and will thrash from 3 to 5 hundred bus (bushels) a day. they put me in mind of a cotton hopper but make a heap more noise and its a right smart machine. that is a hoosier expression out here. you can use if for a by word ...

Activity 8-2: WHY DID PEOPLE LEAVE?

Skills. Interpreting primary source material

Materials. Immigrants' letters in text

Procedure

1. Begin the lesson by asking students to identify reasons why early immigrants came to Iowa. These might include negative factors in their homeland as well as positive benefits of moving to Iowa.

2. Assign different readings to six student volunteers. After the students have read each paragraph aloud, discuss the reasons why settlers came to Iowa.

3. Conclude the lesson by comparing this 19th-century immigration with today. What factors would lead people to leave other parts of the world to settle in Iowa?

Activity 8-3: PATHWAYS TO IOWA

Skills. Identifying and researching family history

Materials. Classroom map of the world, yarn markers

Procedure

1. Introduce the lesson by reviewing with students the fact that all Iowans have ancestors who immigrated from another part of the world (print out the different time scale for American Indians). Using the last names of students, identify the various cultural groups from which students come.

2. Encourage students to collect information on their family histories and report back to the class.

3. Conclude the lesson by displaying a classroom map of the world. Have students identify countries from which their ancestors came, by pinning yarn on the map from Iowa to the various countries.

Activity 8-4: PUSH-PULL AT WORK

Skills. Skimming written material for specific details

Materials. Student copies of handout 8-4

Procedure

1. Begin the lesson by reviewing the push-pull concept. Have students suggest reasons why immigrants left other countries to come to Iowa.

2. Distribute copies of handout 8-4. Have students use their textbooks and other resource materials to identify specific groups and the reasons they came to America.

3. Conclude the lesson by sharing responses as a class.

Name _____

PUSH-PULL AT WORK

Group	Push: Reasons for leaving homeland	Pull: Reasons for coming to Iowa

Activity 8-5: BUXTON: AN IOWA SETTLEMENT

Skills. Reading and interpreting primary source materials

Materials. Minnie London's recollections of Buxton (in text), classroom wall map of Iowa

Procedure

1. Introduce the lesson by reviewing the textbook material on Buxton.
2. Introduce reading by providing students with the following background information on Minnie London.

Mrs. Minnie London was for many years a schoolteacher in Buxton. She vividly recalled her life in Buxton and wrote her recollection titled "As I Remember" many years after leaving the community. Her daughter, Vaeletta Fields, lived for many years in Waterloo. Despite her degree from the University of Iowa, Mrs. Fields was unable to get a good job because she was black. Mrs. London's account carefully describes the unusual setting which existed in Buxton for black workers in the early twentieth century.

3. Read the selection together.
4. Next have students attempt to locate Buxton on the classroom map of Iowa. (Buxton no longer exists. It was located just south of Oskaloosa.)
5. Discuss the following questions:

a. From what states and countries did people come to live and work in the mines near Buxton?
b. Besides coal-mining-related occupations, what other jobs were held by residents of Buxton?
c. How was the community of Buxton a very favorable place for blacks to live? For what reasons did residents of Buxton leave?

PRIMARY SOURCE MATERIAL: "As I Remember:" An Account of Buxton by Minnie B. London (unabridged)

[Note: Mrs. London's memoir is cut considerably in the text.]

In the early spring of 1891 I went as a bride to what was once old Muchakinock, an Indian name that was derived from a nearby creek meaning, I was told, "hard to cross." It was a mining camp five or six miles from Oskaloosa, the county seat.

The camp, as it was called, had formerly been inhabited by white miners. When they went on a strike the Chicago and Northwestern Coal Company, who owned the mines, brought in colored miners and their families from Stauton, Charlottesville, and other towns Virginia. These colored men knew nothing of mining but were taught coal-mining by men hired by the Company. Besides the colored people there were also a goodly number of Swedes.

A branch of C. and N. W. Railroad ran west through the town, which was often used as a street especially in muddy weather.

The coal company not only owned the mines but owned and operated a General Merchandise store, which had a system known as Order Days running, say, from the first to the fifth of the month according to the number of people and the division of the town. On these days the miners or their wives would order groceries, etc., supposedly to last a month or until the next Order Day. To the clerks it meant work and more work, for many times they would have to work all night putting up orders with no extra pay. To the women it was like a great social gathering where they could get together and visit or learn the latest news of the town, perhaps the death of a miner caused by falling slate or the birth of twins having been brought into the world by Old Lady Ross, the midwife of the town, who in her black and white apron was usually kept busy.

The new camp was named Buxton, after the Superintendent of the Mines, a name that was destined for more than a score of years to take its place among other towns of the state. It carried with it all the traditions of the old town, yet it attracted many people from various towns and cities of Illinois, Ohio, Kentucky, and Missouri, in fact from everywhere.

I am sure I am safe in saying that when the town, Buxton, was at its height, no other town in Iowa could boast so many professional and business people of our own group. Doctors, lawyers, teachers, druggists, pharmacists, undertakers, postmaster, Justice of the Peace, constables, clerks, members of the school board, and what have you were all there.

The following persons were prominent at some time in the camp and the positions they held: Dr. E. A. Carter now of Detroit, Michigan; Dr. C. G. Robinson of Chicago; Dr. Williams; Dr. H. H. London, and Dr. Taylor; Lawyers, Geo. W. Woodson and Jas. Spears; Druggists and Pharmacists, B. F. Cooper and Ike and Hattie Hutchinson; Undertaker, S. Billings; Postmaster, Ed Mills; Dentist, L. R. Willis; Music teachers, Cora Thomas, Josie Meadows, Mollie Tibbs, Mrs. Will Lee, and Mrs. Dumond (wife of the Congregational Minister); Justice of the Peace, E. A. London; Constable, Tom Romans. James Roberts manufactured Cuban Hand Made Havana Cigars and did a wholesale and retail business.

The Granberry Bros., manufacturers of tailor made clothes satisfied the most discriminating customer.

Peter Abington, the caterer, kept his wagon on the street all day long selling ice cream, pies, bread, butter, and eggs.

The Buxton Savings Bank occupied one end of the store building with Mrs. Lottie Baxter, the daughter of H. A. Armstrong, as cashier.

Among other business ventures in Buxton that stand out in my memory are: Lewis Reasby with his hamburger and hot dog stand across from the company store and in front of the Y.M.C.A. His comical manner of crying his wares would attract passers-by, who would stop and listen to him, then find themselves thrusting their hands into their pockets and saying, "A hot dog please."

Yes, Buxton had a newspaper too, namely the "Buxton Advocate." It was a weekly edited and owned by R. B. Montgomery.

The Y.M.C.A. was large three-story structure built diagonally across from the company store. It was built expressly for the colored miners, and when they seemed reluctant to take advantage of the opportunity, the Supt. indicated that he would turn it over to the white people. Our people, after reconsideration, pledged cooperation and then a very efficient secretary in the person of L. E. Johnson was engaged.

"Sharp End," I suppose, was the sudden termination of the town to the south, and located in this area was a drug store owned and operated by Ike Hutchinson, whose wife Hattie was the registered pharmacist.

Following the road a little farther west was a grocery store managed by J. W. Neely, who also was a pharmacist. By all means we must not forget H. D. (Hustler) Williams looking out for business.

Near the depot Anderson Perkins and Son operated a hotel and confectionary. They advertised good meals and first class service. Hotel rates $1.00 and $1.50.

The schools took the name of the streets, if we may call them streets, on which they were located or the section of town. Thus we had a Fifth Street School, an Eleventh Street School, and a Swede Town School. They were two-story buildings of four rooms each, thus employing twelve teachers.

The rooms were all well filled with pupils and often a teacher would have to instruct several grades. The grade work done in these schools compared favorably with any in the state. For instance, whenever pupils from these schools went to school in other places, I have been told by the teachers of other towns that they were always glad to get the Buxton children because of their thoroughness.

After several years the number of pupils to enter High School became greater so the School Board erected a large building east of the Fifth Street School maintaining two years of High School to begin with. They employed a Prof. Gilliam as Superintendent. After one year of occupancy it burned down just the Sunday before the beginning of the first semester of the second year. The cause of the loss was said to have been due to the construction of the building. It was never rebuilt so to other towns in the state High School pupils had to continue to go.

About 1921 many of the pioneers were destined to be moved to another coal field as the mines at Buxton were just about worked out. The new camp was called Haydock, still in Monroe County about eighteen miles distant over hills and valleys. Fewer still were willing to follow up the unstable life of a miner and so many continued to go to various cities. The camp had already been populated by many white miners and their families, mainly from Illinois, thus there were less colored people and very few business ventures.

FROM: Minnie B. London. 1940. "As I Remember." Hubert L. Olin Papers. Des Moines: State Historical Society of Iowa.

9 Providing a Government

CONTENT OBJECTIVES

Following the completion of the readings and activities for this chapter, students will have acquired the following understandings:

a. A region cannot arbitrarily become a state on its own. It must first be a district and a territory before it becomes a state.
b. Iowa's territorial and state capitals were moved from Burlington to Iowa City to Des Moines.
c. Iowa became a state on December 28, 1846.
d. As Iowa's population grew, counties were set up to provide for local government.
e. Iowa's first constitution of 1846 was replaced by a new constitution in 1857.
f. Two political parties, the Democrats and the Republicans, have influenced politics in Iowa for 150 years.

VOCABULARY TO KNOW

amendment	elections
Burlington	governor
caucus	The House of Representatives
Congress	Iowa City
constitution	Iowa Territory
The Council	legislature
counties	political parties
Democrats	Republicans
Des Moines	term
district	Wisconsin Territory

FOR FURTHER STUDY

Dorothy Schwieder provides an overview of statehood and the boundary issue in her book, *Iowa: The Middle Land,* published by Iowa State University Press, 1996. Chapter 1, Section 2, "Exploration, Early Settlement and Political Development."

REFERENCES

Bonney, Margaret, ed. "Government for Iowa." *The Goldfinch.* Iowa City: State Historical Society of Iowa, Spring 1976.

_____ ,ed. "The Shape of the State." *The Goldfinch* 4, no.3. Iowa City: State Historical Society of Iowa, February 1983.

_____ ,ed. "Capitals and Capitols." *The Goldfinch* 5, no.4. Iowa City: State Historical Society of Iowa, April 1984.

Noun, Louise R. *Strong-Minded Women.* Ames: Iowa State University Press, 1969.

Sage, Leland L. "Preterritorial and Territorial Iowa 1833-1838-1846." In *A History of Iowa.* Ames: Iowa State University Press, 1974. Chap. 4.

Schlup, Leonard. "Republican Loyalist: James F. Wilson and Party Politics, 1855-1895." *The Annals of Iowa* 52, no. 2 (Spring 1993). Iowa City: State Historical Society of Iowa.

Schwieder, Dorothy. "Exploration, Early Settlement and Political Development." In *Iowa: The Middle Land."* Iowa State University Press, 1996. Chapter 1.

Walker, David. "A Regulated Society." *The Palimpsest* 69, no. 2 (Spring 1988). Iowa City: State Historical Society of Iowa.

Activity 9-1: TRACING IOWA'S CAPITAL CITIES

Skills. Interpreting factual information

Materials. Student copies of handout 9-1, Iowa road maps

Procedure

1. Introduce the lesson by reviewing the progression of events which led to Iowa's statehood:

1803-Louisiana is purchased from France
1834-Iowa becomes part of Michigan Territory
1836-Iowa becomes part of Wisconsin Territory
1838-Iowa Territory is established
1846-Iowa becomes a state

2. Distribute copies of handout 9-1. Provide time for students to complete this activity using information found in the text and the Iowa road maps.

3. Conclude the lesson by sharing student responses. Discussion should focus on the relationship between the capital's location and the progressive development of Iowa in a westward direction.

Name _____

TRACING IOWA'S CAPITAL CITIES

Directions. Fill in the following blanks using information found in the textbook and an Iowa road map.

Burlington   _____   _____
                              (county)   (years)

Reason for being selected as Iowa's capital: _____

_____

_____

Iowa City   _____   _____
                              (county)   (years)

Reason for being selected as Iowa's capital: _____

_____

_____

Des Moines   _____   _____
                              (county)   (years)

Reason for being selected as Iowa's capital: _____

_____

_____

10 Schools for a New State

CONTENT OBJECTIVES

Following the completion of the readings and activities for this chapter, students will have acquired the following understandings:

a. As soon as the first settlers arrived in Iowa, schools were set up for the education of children.
b. Early Iowa schools were scheduled to accommodate the needs of children from farm families.
c. Later high schools and academies were built to meet the needs of older students.
d. Around 1900 some schools began to consolidate to offer better educational programs.
e. The State of Iowa and many religious groups set up colleges and universities.

VOCABULARY TO KNOW

academy	Land Ordinance of 1785
Chautauqua	*McGuffey's Readers*
consolidation	property tax
grammar school	subscription schools

PEOPLE TO IDENTIFY

Dr. Isaac Galland	William H. McGuffey
Berryman Jennings	Puritans

FOR FURTHER STUDY

1. Visit a reconstructed country school in your area. Many county or local historical societies across the state have been instrumental in preserving this part of Iowa's history. Provide students with an opportunity to observe and experience education in a one-room school.

2. Have a member of the local school board visit the classroom. Have students prepared to ask questions about his/her duties and the organization of the local school board.

REFERENCES

Bonney, Margaret, ed. "Going to School in Iowa." *The Goldfinch* 2, no.4 (April 1981). Iowa City: State Historical Society of Iowa.

Cooper, Arnie. "A Stony Road: Black Education in Iowa, 1838-1860." *The Annals of Iowa* 48, nos. 3, 4 (Winter/Spring 1986). Iowa City: State Historical Society of Iowa.

1870 Iowa State Almanac. Explorations in Iowa History Project. Cedar Falls: Malcolm Price Laboratory School, University of Northern Iowa.

Johnson, Keach. "The State of Elementary and Secondary Education in Iowa in 1900." *The Annals of Iowa* 49, nos. 1 & 2 (Summer/Fall 1987). Iowa City: State Historical Society of Iowa.

Schwieder, Dorothy. "Religious and Educational Institutions in Iowa: Establishing the Foundations." In *Iowa: The Middle Land.* Iowa State University Press, 1996. Chapter 1.

Swaim, Ginalie. "An Acre of Hill." *The Palimpsest* 67, no. 1 (Spring 1987). Iowa City: State Historical Society of Iowa.

Activity 10-1: COUNTRY SCHOOL MEMORIES

Skills. Collecting information from a personal interview

Materials. Student copies of handout 10-1

Procedure

1. Based on the reading of the material on education, discuss the differences students perceive between Iowa schools today and those in years past.

2. As a class, identify people students know who attended one-room or country schools. (Most one-room schools in Iowa were not in use after 1960.) Many older relatives would vividly recall this experience.

3. Propose a project to interview a person who attended a country school. Distribute copies of handout 10-1. Read and discuss the four questions suggested on the sheet. Have students suggest at least three other questions they might ask the person they are interviewing.

4. When students have completed their interviews, provide class time for sharing and displaying interview results.

Interviewer _____

Name _____

Date _____

1. Where did you go to country school?

_____

2. For how many years did you attend country school? _____

3. How many other students were in your grade? _____

4. What activities or lessons were included in a typical school day? _____

_____

5. _____

_____

_____

6. _____

_____

_____

7. _____

_____

_____

8. _____

_____

_____

Activity 10-2: COUNTRY SCHOOL SCHEDULE

Skills. Comparing two sources of information

Materials. Overhead projector, blank transparencies, markers, student copies of handout 10-2

Procedure

1. Introduce the lesson by reviewing the fact that nineteenth-century schools had a different schedule and list of courses than we generally have today. Using the overhead projector, have students assist in listing a daily schedule of courses for the class.

2. Distribute copies of handout 10-2. Have students copy their daily schedule in the right column using the information projected on the overhead screen. (The class schedule for 1870 can also be found in the textbook.)

3. Compare the 1870 schedule with the class schedule, noting similarities and differences.

Class Schedule 1870		My Class Schedule
9:00 a.m.	Opening Exercises	
	Lord's Prayer	
	Patriotic Poems and Axioms	
9:15 a.m.	Roll	
9:20 a.m.	Reading	
9:40 a.m.	Mental Arithmetic	
10:10 a.m.	Geography and Mapping	
10:35 a.m.	Recess	
10:50 a.m.	Written Arithmetic	
11:15 a.m.	History and Our Constitution	
11:45 a.m.	Meal Break and Recess	
1:30 p.m.	Reading	
2:00 p.m.	Physical Geography	
2:30 p.m.	Grammar	
3:15 p.m.	Blackboard Exercise	
3:30 p.m.	Recess for Day	

SOURCE: *1870 Iowa State Almanac,* Explorations on Iowa History Project, Price Laboratory School, University of Northern Iowa, 1979, p. 33.

Activity 10-3: COUNTRY SCHOOL DAY

Skills. Cooperative group planning

Materials. A camera and film to record the day's events

Procedure

1. Introduce the lesson by reviewing what students have learned about going to school in a country school.

2. Propose a project where students would plan a country school day for the class. The following items would need to be considered:

room arrangement	lunch
schedule	assignments
dress	classroom materials

After assigning specific jobs to committees or individuals, allow time for students to plan the country school day. Students may wish to dress in pioneer-type clothing, bring a lunch to school, and arrange the room to include a recitation bench, cloak "room", and dunce's corner. Students may also wish to invite parents and/ or other classes to attend a country school "program" to be put on at the end of the day. A typical program would include plays, recitations, and of course, refreshments.

3. If pictures are taken, a scrapbook or bulletin board display might be created to highlight the major events of the day.

11 Keeping the Faith on the Frontier

CONTENT OBJECTIVES

Following the completion of the readings and activities for this chapter, students will have acquired the following understandings:

a. Many of Iowa's early religious groups were closely tied to cultural or nationality groups that settled n Iowa.
b. Catholic and Protestant Christians were the dominant religious groups on the Iowa frontier.
c. Latter Day Saints, often called Mormons, crossed southern and central Iowa on their way to the West. Some stayed to become the first white settlers in southwest Iowa.
d. Activities of religious groups provided cohesiveness for Iowa's early communities.
e. Iowa's religious groups have been active in many social causes.

VOCABULARY TO KNOW

American Missionary Society	Lutheran
Amish	Methodist
Catholic	Mormon
circuit riders	Mormon Trail
Congregationalist	Nauvoo, Illinois
denomination	Presbyterian
diocese	Quaker
Iowa Band	Reformed Church
Jewish	religion

PEOPLE TO IDENTIFY

Father Samuel Mazzuchelli   Joseph Smith

Mathias Loras   Rev. Asa Turner

FOR FURTHER STUDY

1. Most religious groups in Iowa are Protestant or Catholic. Plan a field trip highlighting a lesser-known religious group. Iowa's larger communities will often have a Jewish synagogue, a Greek Orthodox church, or a Mormon church. Contact the church to arrange a tour and invite a speaker.

2. Invite a black gospel singer to perform and interpret several spirituals for the class. Most traditional spirituals originated in slave days and contained an immediate as well as a spiritual message.

REFERENCES

Gutjahr, Paul. "'Hundreds of Souls Lie in the Balance:' An Eastern Congregational Minister Ponders Moving West to Iowa." *The Palimpsest* 74, no. 2 (Summer 1993). Iowa City: State Historical Society of Iowa.

Hartley, William G. "Mormons and Early Iowa History (1838 to 1858): Eight Distinct Conditions." *The Annals of Iowa* 59, no. 3 (Summer 2000). Iowa City: State Historical Society of Iowa.

Jorgensen, Danny L. "The Cutlerites of Southwestern Iowa: A Latter-day Saint Schism and its Role in the Early Settlement of Iowa." *The Annals of Iowa* 58, no. 2 (Spring 1999). Iowa City: State Historical Society of Iowa.

Journal of Archer Walters. Explorations in Iowa History Project. Cedar Falls: Malcolm Price Laboratory School, University of Northern Iowa.

Launius, Roger D. "The Mormon Quest for a Perfect Society at Lamoni, Iowa, 1870-1890." *The Annals of Iowa* 47, no. 4 (Spring 1984). Iowa City: State Historical Society of Iowa.

Miller, Henry A. "Methodist Revival Meeting: Remembering Boyhood Experience in 1865." *The Palimpsest* 71, no. 1 (Spring 1990). Iowa City: State Historical Society of Iowa.

Schwieder, Dorothy. "Religious and Educational Institutions in Iowa: Establishing the Foundations." In *Iowa: The Middle Land.* Iowa State University Press, 1996. Chapter 2.

Activity 11-1: JOURNAL OF ARCHER WALTERS

Skills. Interpreting primary source materials

Materials. Student copies of handout 11-1

Procedure

1. Introduce the lesson by reviewing the section in the textbook on the Mormons.
2. Read and discuss the introduction as a class.

3. Distribute copies of handout 11-1. Provide time for students to complete the questions.

4. Conclude the lesson by discussing the difficulties faced by the Mormons as they sought to establish a community on the frontier.

CROSSING IOWA WITH ARCHER WALTERS

Directions. The answers to the questions about Archer Walters's journey across Iowa are found in his journal or the introduction to it.

BACKGROUND INFORMATION

1. Where was Archer Walters's home? _____

2. What was Archer Walters's destination? _____

3. Who was accompanying Walters on his journey? _____

_____

4. Why was Walters making this trip? _____

_____

5. Who planned the Handcart Expedition?_____

TRAVEL CONDITIONS IN 1856

1. What type of vehicle was used by Walters and the other Mormon migrants?

_____

2. What was the average number of miles traveled by Walters each day? (Add the miles shown in journal entries. Divide by number of days with mileage entries only.) _____

3. How many times did Walters report repairing handcarts? _____

4. How many times did Walters report illnesses? _____

5. How many died as listed in Walters's journal? _____

6. What references were there to the weather in Walters's entries? _____

_____

Activity 11-2: COMMUNITY PROFILE

Skills. Creating a chart

Materials. Chart paper

Procedure

1. Introduce the lesson by listing on the blackboard the various community religious groups as the students identify them.

2. Have students help to plan a strategy to create a religious profile for the community. Specific items might include:

a. Names of religious groups in the community
b. Membership
c. Activities
d. Clergy
e. Social services (rest homes, charities, hospitals, etc.)

Representatives from various groups might be consulted by class members in order to obtain specific information.

3. A chart for display in the classroom could be created by the students to summarize their findings.

Activity 11-3: HISTORY OF LOCAL RELIGIOUS GROUPS

Skills. Conducting a personal interview, using local resources

Materials. None

Procedure

1. Introduce the lesson by reviewing the traditional role which religious groups played in the development of Iowa's early communities. Both the school and the church offered opportunities for community cohesiveness.

2. Have students suggest community resources that might be helpful in identifying the early religious groups in the community and the role they played in the past. Older citizens, the local library, and the historical society will all be helpful in uncovering this information. In addition, many churches will have written a church history as part of a centennial celebration.

3. After specific religious groups have been identified and students have been grouped for work, allow time for students to research and identify the major characteristics of their community groups. The relationship between ethnic groups and religious groups should be investigated. For instance, Danish settlers were almost always Lutheran, and many Danish Lutheran churches maintained Danish services into the 1940s. This concept should not be overemphasized, however. Church groups such as the Methodists were

not as specifically ethnic because of their traditional emphasis on evangelism and outreach.

4. When students have completed their research, provide time for group reports.

PRIMARY SOURCE MATERIAL: Excerpts from the Journal of Archer Walters from Iowa City to the Missouri River (unabridged)

The Mormon migrations to Utah form some of the more colorful chapters of the history of the American frontier. In their search for a safe place to practice their religion, the followers of Joseph Smith moved from settlement to settlement in the Midwest. Finally, in 1846 and 1847, Brigham Young led the Mormons to their new home in the Salt Lake Valley.

Eight years later (1855), Brigham Young planned the migration of 1300 Mormon converts through Iowa. He suggested that they travel between New York City and Iowa City by rail. From Iowa City to Salt Lake City they could travel on foot, moving their families and their goods by pulling handcarts. Archer Walters, a 47-year-old carpenter from Sheffield, England, joined the Handcart Expedition at Iowa City.

June 11, 1856—Journeyed 7 miles. Very dusty. All tried and smothered with dust and camped in the dust or where the dust blowed. Was captain over my tent of 18 in number but they were a family of Welsh and our spirits were not united. Had a tent but Bro. Ellsworth would not let me use it and had to leave my tent poles behind.

June 12—Journeyed 12 miles. Went very fast with our hand carts. Harriet still very ill. ...

June 15—Got up about 4 o'clock to make a coffin for my brother John Lee's son named William Lee, aged 12 years. Meetings Sunday as usual and at the same time had to make another coffin for Sister Prator's child. Was tired with repairing handcarts the last week. Went and buried them by moonlight at Bear Creek.

June 16—Harriet very ill. Traveled 19 miles and after pitching tent mended carts.

June 17—Traveled about 17 miles; pitched tent. Made a little coffin for Bro. Job Welling's son and mended a handcart wheel. ...

June 21—Traveled about 13 miles. Camped at Indian Creek. Bro. Bowers died about 6 o'clock; from Birmingham Conference. Went to buy some wood to make the coffin but the kind farmer gave me the wood and nails. It had been a very hot day and I was never more tired, but God has said as my day my strength shall be.

June 22—Got up at break of day and made the coffin for Bro. James Bowers by 9 o'clock and he was buried at 11 o'clock. Aged 44 years 5 months 2 days. His relatives cried very much after I lifted him in the coffin and waited to screw him down. 11 o'clock washed in the creek and felt very much refreshed. Meeting Sunday 2 o'clock until 7.

June 24—Traveled about 18 miles. Very hot. Bro. Ellsworth being always with a family from Birmingham named Brown and always that tent going first and walking so fast and some fainted by the way. ...

June 26—Traveled about 1 mile. Very faint from lack of food. We are only allowed about 3/4 lb. of flour a head each day and about 3 oz. of sugar each week. About 1/2 of a lb. of bacon each a week; which makes those that have no money very weak. Made a child's coffin for Sister Sheen—Emma Sheen Aged 2 1/2 years.

June 27—Got up before sunrise. Cut a tombstone on wood and bury the child before starting from camp.

June 28— Rose soon after 4 o'clock. Started with high wind. Short of water and I was never more tired. Rested a bit after we camped then came on a thunder storm, and rain, blowed our tent down. Split the canvas and wet our clothes and we had to lay on the wet clothes and ground. ...

June 29—Rather stiff in joints when we rose. ... Busy all day. My wife and Sarah mending. Short of provisions. Children crying for their dinner.

June 30—Rose in good health, except Harriet, and started without handcarts with but little breakfast ... but never traveled 17 miles more easily. ... Sleep very well after prayers in tent.

July 1, 1856—Rose soon. It looked very cloudy and began to rain. Traveled about 15 miles. Walked very fast—nearly 4 miles an hour. Bro. Brown's family and some young sisters with Bro. Ellsworth always going fIrst which causes many of the brothers to have hard feelings ... my children cry with hunger and it grieves me and makes me cross. I can live upon green herbs or anything and do go nearly an day without any and am strengthened with a morsel. Repaired handcarts.

July 3—Ever to be remembered Bro. Card gave me 1/2 dollar for making his daughter's coffin. Start with my cart before the camp as others had done but was told not to and had to suffer for it. Went the wrong way; about 30 of the brothers and sisters, and went 10 1/2 miles the wrong way. We put our three handcarts together and made beds with an the clothes we had and laid down about 1/2 past 10 o'clock. 11 o'clock Brother Butler who had charge of the mule teams came with the mules and wagon to fetch us. Got to camp when they were getting up. Laid down about an hour and started with the camp.

July 5—A deer or elk served out to camp. Brother Parker brings into camp his little boy (age 6) that had been lost (3 days). Great joy right through the camp. The mother's joy I can not describe. Expect we are going to rest. Washing, etc., today. Jordan Creek. Made a pair of sashes for the old farmer. Indian meal; no flour. Slept well.

July 6—Made 2 doors for ... 3 dollars and boarded with farmer.

July 7—Harriet better. Lydia poorly. Traveled about 20 miles.

July 8—Traveled a round about road about 20 miles. Crossed the river Missouri and camped at the city of Florence. Very tired; glad to rest. Slept well. Lydia better and Harriet. All in good spirits. Expect to stop some time. ...

FROM: The *Journal of Archer Walters*. Explorations in Iowa History Project. Cedar Fans: Malcolm Price Laboratory School, University of Northern Iowa.

12 Experiments in Community Living

CONTENT OBJECTIVES

Following the completion of the readings and activities for this chapter, students will have acquired the following understandings:

a. Communitarian groups that settled in Iowa developed their own particular cultural norms and lifestyles that remind us that people of many different points of view have helped to shape Iowa's unique cultural heritage.
b. The Icarians, a communitarian group, existed in Iowa from 1855 to 1895.
c. The Society of True Inspiration settled in Iowa in 1855. The Inspirationists maintained their simple communal lifestyle until 1930 when they reorganized to form the Amana Society.
d. The Old Order Amish settled in Iowa in the 1840s. Although a number of Amish groups have appeared over the years, many live in essentially the same manner as most Iowa farmers did in 1900.

VOCABULARY TO KNOW

Amish Mennonites	duplexes
Beachy Amish	economic
baptism	elders
commercial	Icarians
commitment	independent
communitarian	isolate
conscientious	Old Order Amish
cultural	settlement
depression	Society of True Inspiration
	Werkzeuges

PEOPLE TO IDENTIFY

Barbara Heineman   Jacob Ammann

Etienne Cabet   Maria Marchand Ross

FOR FURTHER STUDY

1. Using a map of the world, have students identify the route some of the communitarians used to get to Iowa. Teachers may wish to make supplementary resource material available to students.

2. Take students on a field trip to the Amanas. If this is not possible, allow time for students who have visited the Amanas to share their experiences.

3. Communitarian groups have settled in other states in addition to Iowa. Individual students may wish to locate information about communitarians outside of Iowa to compare and contrast with information about Iowa groups.

4. Some students will enjoy reading books about communitarians who settled in Iowa and other parts of the United States. One such book, *A Change and a Parting*, by Barbara Yambura, chronicles the events leading to the reorganization of the Society of True Inspiration to form the Amana Society in 1930. Consult the librarian for additional titles.

REFERENCES

Andelson, Jonathan G. "Tradition, Innovation, and Assimilation in Iowa's Amana Colonies." *The Palimpsest* 69, no.1 (Spring 1988). Iowa City: State Historical Society of Iowa.

Hoehnle, Peter. The Great Change: The Reorganization of Amana Society, 1931-1933. Unpublished thesis, Iowa State University, Ames, 1997.

"Iowa's Amish People." *The Goldfinch* (Spring 1975). Iowa City: State Historical Society of Iowa.

Schwieder, Dorothy. "Agrarian Stability in Utopian Societies: A Comparison of Economic Practices of Old Order Amish and Hutterites." In *Patterns and Perspectives in Iowa History,* Dorothy Schwieder, ed. Ames: Iowa State University Press, 1973.

Schwieder, Dorothy. "Cultural Diversity." In *Iowa: The Middle Land."* Iowa State University Press, 1996. Chapter 11.

Schwieder, Elmer and Dorothy. *A Peculiar People: Iowa's Old Order Amish.* Ames: Iowa State University Press, 1975.

Smith, Martha Browning. "The Story of Icaria." In *Patterns and Perspectives in Iowa History,* Dorothy Schwieder, ed. Ames: Iowa State University Press, 1973.

Yambura, Barbara. *A Change and a Parting.* Ames: Iowa State University Press, 1960.

Activity 12-1: THE OLD ORDER AMISH

Skills. Interpreting photographs

Materials. Study prints of Amish men in conversation, Amish threshing and Amish barn-raising (in text).

Procedure

1. Introduce the lesson by reviewing information from the text regarding the origin and development of Amish communities.

2. Examine the three study prints illustrating various aspects of Amish life.

3. After providing students time to view the prints, discuss the following questions:

a. When might the photographs have been taken?
b. What does each photograph reveal about the Amish way of life?
c. In what way does the Amish lifestyle differ from yours?
d. Why have the Amish held on to their way of life while the world has continued to change rapidly?

Activity 12-2: *THE BUDGET*, AN AMISH MENNONITE NEWSPAPER

Skills. Working in small groups, interpreting information in newspaper articles

Materials. Student copies of handouts 12-2a (also in text), 12-2b, 12-2c, and 12-2d

Procedure

1. Begin the lesson by reviewing that the Amish maintain a strong sense of community and belonging among their members. One way the community ties at large are strengthened is through the Amish Mennonite newspaper. *The Budget,* printed in Sugarcreek, Ohio, devotes a large section in each issue to everyday information from local fellowships throughout the Americas.

2. Divide students into four groups. Provide each group with copies of one of the handouts. Each handout includes samples of the Iowa section of *The Budget.* Encourage students to read the entries and categorize the kinds of information that are often included in the paper.

3. Conclude the lesson by having each group share its findings. Discuss the value of *The Budget* as a unifying vehicle of communication for the Amish Mennonite community.

This activity can be adapted to use the columns of *The Budget* given in the textbook.

KEOTA, IOWA

Salem Mennonite Fellowship

Apr. 17--A sunny pleasant morning.

Tues. supper guests of John Mark Millers were the Philip Martin family of Boyd, Wisc. They spent the night at Walter Beachys'.

Fri. p.m. a number of sisters met at the church kitchen to make an abundant supply of noodles for our Belize mission workers.

Jesse Millers attended the funeral on Sun. of a stepbrother, Jacob J. Miller at Plain City, Ohio. Jesse's sisters, Viola Gingerich and Anna Mae Beachy, went along.

Visitors in church Sun. (morning and evening) were Paul Hostetlers and dau. of Mt. View, Ark. They were here visiting in his parents' home, the Emmet Hostetlers'.

Council meeting was held Sun. morning in preparation for communion service in two weeks.

Wilford Stutzman drove his pickup pulling a small house trailer down to Seymour, Mo. are Mon. They are planning to put a camper on the pickup, and is to be driven to Belize by the Edwin Miller family of Summersville, Mo. The Millers expect to replace the David Stutzmans while they are home on furlough, starting in May. Davids plan to come home via the camper; the house trailer is to be used by the James Yoders as a supplement to their native house.

Martha Stoddard is having a checkup with her doctor in Iowa City today.

Rachel Stutzman has been helping out in the Stoddard home, preparing meals and being with Martha so Glen can be out. She can go home at night. Mary E. Bender's back problem flared up so she is not at the Stoddards' at present.

Mrs. Alton Miller

KALONA, IOWA

April 16--The weather remains cool, cloudy and damp.

Anna Laura, the 8-year-old daughter of Edward and Ida (Miller) Schlabach, had an operation for appendicitis, on Saturday.

Yesterday, Willis, son of Daniel C. Masts of Coalgate, Okla. and Gloria, daughter of Pre. Mark A. Millers, were published for marriage. The wedding is to be May 10th. Willis has been living with us for over 2 years already, so he is about like our son. He is farming our place this year, so I guess we will also get a daughter!

Mrs. John N. Borntrager and children of Anabel, Mo. were here last week to visit her parents, John S. Yoder Jrs.

Saturday was the sale of the household goods of Miss Lena M. Yoder, at the property in Kalona. Lena is with her niece, Mrs. Edna Yoder, for several years already, and no one was in her house. She sold the house recently, and Lydia May Yoder will move into it before long. Lena had some old fashioned things which brought fancy prices. The glass cupboard brought over $500; a small earthen pot around $70, a small kerosene lamp, $80, nice china dishes, around $18 each. A 4 piece set of creamer, sugar bowl, spoon holder and butter dish went for $125.

Andy Helmuths and Irvin Gingerichs returned home Wednesday from their winter's stay in Florida. John R. Knepps returned home from Florida last week.

Mrs. Tobe Detweiler, Mrs. Amos Mast and daughter Salina and Mrs. Levi Yoder of Jamesport, Mo. were visitors in this community last week. Mrs. Yoder visited her aged mother, Mrs. Barbara Chupp and the others had come to visit Mrs. John S. Yoder Jr.

M. E. G.

KALONA, IOWA

Apr. 9—After several nice days last week, we are having wet weather. It rained nearly all day yesterday. Field work is at a standstill; some oats was put in the ground last week.

Churches on the 22nd are to be in the M. Dale Miller and Joe Coblentz homes.

Cephas Yoders, Eli S. Bontragers, Ben L. Yoders, Tobie Millers, Jonas J. Beachy, Mrs. Ernest Yoder, Henry H. Yoder, Mrs. Wm. G. Hochstetler, David and Susanna Gingerich attended the funeral of Mrs. Andy Kurtz in Buchanan Co. on Fri.

Henry M. Miller, Steven Millers, John C. Helmuths, Solomon Yoder, Isaac Hershbergers, Enos H. Millers, Mrs. Anna Yoder, Ivan Bender and Dan J. Shetler went to Springs, Pa. to attend the funeral of Samuel Bender, which was today.

Alton and Emanuel Borntragers, Eli M. Ellis and Vera Borntrager, Marvin and Ivan Borntrager, Tobie Miller, Henry E. Bender, Vernon E. Bontrager, John and James and Jonas Beachy (driver) were to Clark, Mo. on Wed. to attend Jakie Gingerich's sale.

Lester and Ab Coblentzes were to Ill. over the weekend to attend the funeral of Herb Miller.

Pre. Lester B. Miller was admitted to the hospital today where he is to have surgery on Wed. He again has a tumor in his head.

Edwin Ropps and Mrs. Eldon Nisley were to leave this afternoon for Evansville, Wisc. to attend a wedding tomorrow.   M.E.G.

LEON, IOWA

Apr. 18—Sun is shining and forecast is for warmer weather. So far no field work was done due to wet weather.

Early Sat. morning another son was born to Joni and Ruby Stutzman. They named him Adrain Jon. He has 2 sisters and 2 brothers. Ruby's mother, Mrs. Fannie Miller from Kalona, is there to help out.

Melvin Yoders and sons were visiting from Thomas, Okla. at their sister's, the Alva Yoders'. They made a stop at John Yutzys' Sat. p.m.

Quite a number of people from Kalona were down for Moses Yoder's Beefalo sale yesterday. Their son Jake and family, Andy Helmuth and wife, Linneus, Jake and Willard Gingerich and wives, Dave Mast and wife, Lizzie Gingerich, Elmer Schrock and wife and some cousins and friends.

John Stoltzfus from Kennedyville, Md. flew in Mon. p.m. to help his brother Ivan get started on his roof coating business. They are working in Trenton, Mo. at present.

Myron and Loretta Yoder, Duane Troyer, Andy Ray Chupp and Omar Miller returned home from their eastern trip Fri. evening. Omar had flown to Fla. from Washington, D.C. and met the others Fri. morning in Plain City, Ohio area. Andy Ray left Sat. morning for his home in Okla.   Mrs. Andy Miller

BLOOMFIELD, IOWA

May 8--Weather remains cool, but with a few more drying days farmers will be getting into the fields. No corn planted so far except sweet corn.

Our church was at Ervin Jay Masts' and to be at Henry D. Yoders' next time.

The redbuds are beginning to bloom here now. Over the 28th went to Marshfield, Mo. which is further south and on the way down we saw hundreds of redbuds in full bloom.

Emma and Amanda Miller attended a special school at Centerville. Recently while at school, Emma fell and broke her arm. She spent some time at the hospital but is on the mend now.

A number of people have written to inquire about the fast growing broilers I wrote about. They are available from quite a few different hatcheries. Some call them meatmakers. Our hatchery calls them Cornish Cross. They are a cross between Cornish and white rocks and all they do is eat and grow. Three pounds of feed should produce one pound of meat and they grow so fast they can hardly walk. I didn't say all of our weighed 5 lbs. at 6 weeks, only the biggest ones.

Yesterday our very close friends, Marvin and Carolyn Priest and 4 children from Greencastle, Pa. (formerly from Hagerstown, Md.) came to see us. Unfortunately they had trouble with their van, so we were late for church. They took our car home and Vernon plans to fix their van, then we'll swap again. Marvin told me that we were going to bring it up Fri. and stay until Sun. Sounds great!

Mrs. Vernon Martin

KALONA, IOWA
Sharon Bethel News

May 8--We actually passed a weekend without getting any rain, which gives the ground a chance to dry off once. Farmers are getting very anxious to get their crops planted.

Mrs. Fannie Miller came home last week, after helping out at the Joni Stutzmans' in Leon, Ia. for two weeks. Lynn Helmuths and family went to Leon, Ia. for the weekend.

Mrs. John I: Helmuth remains about the same. She gets around with a walker and moves very slowly. After going a very short distance, her breathing is so hard it moves her whole body, until she sits awhile. She has not been in church for some time.

Yesterday our school went to Cedar Rapids on a field trip. They had a cold day. Today is their last day for this term. Sat. we plan to have the school picnic.

Irene and Henry Schrock left this morning for Hillcrest Home in Ark. where Irene plans to start a term of service, and Henry (along with some other former Hillcresters) plans to go to Colo. for a two-week camping trip. Sunday evening after church the youth gathered at the Henry Bontragers' to have a farewell for Irene.

John N. Miller from the Haven Congregation, was the guest speaker at our church Sunday evening.

Gordon & Dorothy Hershberger

LEON, IOWA

March 6—A nice sunny day but temperature was 10 above this morning. Some folks already planted early garden.

Last Wednesday was the grand opening of the Leon Sale Barn. A dentist from Paris, Mo. purchased it for his son and his wife, just a young married couple. Homer Hershbergers and girls operate the cafe part.

Simon and Ida Mullet from Kalona, on the way home from Phoenix, Arizona where they spent the winter, stopped at the home of Moses Yoders' on Saturday for dinner. Ida is a sister to Cora.

Ray Yutzys and children and Homer and Susie Hershberger spent Sunday in Kalona to attend M.D.S. meeting.

Enos and Polly Mast returned home Friday morning. They were gone over 3 weeks. They were to Kansas, Missouri and Marion, Kentucky where they encountered a lot of snow. They had to be taken by buggy to where they wanted to visit as roads weren't opened yet.

Joas and Katie Mast and their son Alberts and family spent Saturday in Jamesport, Mo. area to shop and visit Katie's brother Harrys and family.

Mose Yoders and sons, Jrs. and family, Enoses and family and Jonases and girls were at Perry Bontragers' for Sunday dinner and to celebrate the February birthdays and also Mose and Cora's 47th anniversary.

Yesterday morning breakfast visitors with Perry Bontragers were Mrs. Eldon Bontrager and daughter Carolyn from Kansas, Mrs. (Tobe) Mattie Miller, and Eli Bontragers from Kalona. They were on the way to Kansas.

Last evening a birthday surprise was sprung on the writer. Those here were Joas and Katie and Enos and Polly Mast, John and Sylvia Yutzys, Mose and Cora Yoder and Simon, Vina, Loretta and John Yoder and Shawn Troyer, Darla and Juanita Stoltzfus, Ivan Stoltzfus and Myron Yoder.

Morris Yoder is expected home today from his Europe and Holy Land tour.

Mrs. Andy Miller

DALLAS CENTER, IOWA

March 8—Our meeting on Sunday was at the Brother Philip Funk home. Min. Philip brought the main sermon. The young married couples all stayed for dinner. We also had prayer meeting at Philip's home on Wednesday evening.

John and Edna Myers are planning on having a sale on Saturday of their surplus household goods and yard and garden equipment. They are nicely settled in a retirement apt. in Dallas Center.

Uncle John Wingert had a mild heart attack last Thursday. He seems to be coming along quite well and has been moved to a special care room. Uncle John is 77 and I can never remember of him being sick. He is always active and since his retirement he is the handy fix-it man for lots of folks.

Daphene McGlothin spent several days of her spring break with her sister Nitavonne at Rochester, Minnesota. Nitavonne is a nurse at the St. Mary's Hospital in the coronary care unit.

On Saturday Louise and Anna Keller, Fannie Fox, Dorothy Hawbaker and I decided to remind Ruth Meyers of her birthday by taking her to Duff's to eat and visiting the Botanical Center.

Mrs. Stanley Funk

Activity 12-3: ICARIAN SETTLEMENT

Skills. Reading and interpreting a map

Materials. Map of Icarian settlement (in text), student copies of handout 12-3

Procedure

1. Introduce the lesson by reviewing the chapter material related to the Icarian settlement.

2. Locate the map of Icaria in the text, distribute copies of handout 12-3. Provide students with time to complete the questions accompanying the map.

3. Conclude the lesson by discussing student responses.

ICARIAN SETTLEMENT

Directions. Use the map of Icaria to answer the following questions.

1. What year does the map represent? For how many years had the Icarians been in Iowa?

_____

2. How can you tell that the Icarians shared things? _____

_____

3. For what reasons might the Icarians have settled near the Nodaway River? _____

_____

4. What kinds of work did the Icarians do for a living? _____

_____

5. What methods of transportation might the Icarians have used? _____

_____

6. What kinds of activities did the children do? _____

_____

7. List the different types of tools the Icarians used on their settlement. _____

_____

_____

8. What different forms of energy did the Icarians probably use? _____

_____

_____

Activity 12-4: THREE IOWA COMMUNITARIAN SOCIETIES

Skills. Using the textbook to compare and contrast three social groups

Materials. Student copies of handout 12-4

Procedure

1. Introduce the lesson by briefly reviewing information from the chapter regarding each of the three major communitarian societies: the Old Order Amish, the Icarians, and the Society of True Inspiration.

2. Divide the class into three groups and distribute copies of handout 12-4. Provide time for each group to complete the worksheet for one of the three communitarian societies.

3. Conclude the lesson by sharing responses and comparing the characteristics of each group.

Name _____

THREE IOWA COMMUNITARIAN SOCIETIES

	Icarians	Society of True Inspiration	Old Order Amish
Important Push Factors			
Important Pull Factors			
Where Settled			
Religion			
Work Activities			
Role of Children			
Importance Today			

Directions. Use information from the textbook to complete each of the boxes.

Activity 12-5: UNDERSTANDING COMMUNAL LIFE

Skills. Working together as a group

Materials. None

Procedure

1. Introduce the lesson by having students identify classroom jobs and responsibilities necessary for keeping the room running smoothly. In addition, inform students that for a day all property within the classroom will be held in common by the class. All crayons will be kept in a common box for the class to use. All scissors, books, pencils, etc., will be held as common property. Several jobs within the class will be assigned to individuals.

2. After adequate planning time, have a community day within the classroom where property and responsibility are held jointly by the class members.

3. Debrief this activity the following day by discussing the positive and negative aspects of a communal lifestyle. Relate this discussion to the successes and failures of Iowa's historic communal societies, as well as communal properties in today's society, such as libraries, parks, recreation centers, and museums.

13 Life on the Farm—Iowa Style

CONTENT OBJECTIVES

Following the completion of the readings and activities for this chapter, students will have acquired the following understandings:

a. Corn and hogs were Iowa's main farm products following the Civil War.
b. Farm work varied with the seasons and required cooperation among families and neighbors.
c. Many technological advances began to profoundly affect farm production and farm life.
d. After 1920 farmers faced two decades of economic difficulty.

VOCABULARY TO KNOW

agriculture	haying
butchering	industry
canning	lye
cultivating	Mason jars
diversified farming	Rural Free Delivery (RFD)
harvesting	threshing

FOR FURTHER STUDY

1. Visit the Living History Farms near Des Moines. Various stages of agricultural development are beautifully illustrated through the farm displays.
2. Visit a farm as a class. Provide students with the opportunity to observe the operation of the farm as well as the business aspects of running a farm.

REFERENCES

Bonney, Margaret, ed. "Come to the Fair!" *The Goldfinch* 5, no.1 (September 1983). Iowa City: State Historical Society of Iowa.

Graber, William Bernard. "A Farm Family Enters the Modern World." *The Palimpsest* 68, no.2 (Summer 1987). Iowa City: State Historical Society of Iowa.

Hein, Ruth. "A Town Girl Becomes a Farm Helper." *The Palimpsest* 71, no. 2 (Summer 1990). Iowa City: State Historical Society of Iowa.

Marshall, Gordon. "Hired Men, Iowa's Unsung Farm Resource." *The Palimpsest* 74, no. 4 (Winter 1993). Iowa City: State Historical Society of Iowa.

Meusberger, Joanne. "Farm Girl." *The Palimpsest* 68, no. 4; and 69, no. 1 (Winter 1987/Spring 1988). Iowa City: State Historical Society of Iowa.

Peterson, Fred W. "Tradition and Change in Nineteenth-Century Iowa Farmhouses." *The Annals of Iowa* 52, no. 3 (Summer 1993). Iowa City: State Historical Society of Iowa.

Salvaneschi, Lenore. "Harvest Time." *The Palimpsest* 65, no.6 (November/December 1984). Iowa City: State Historical Society of Iowa.

Schwieder, Dorothy. "A Home First and a Business Second: Agriculture and Farm Life in the Middle Years." In *Iowa: The Middle Land.* Iowa State University Press, 1996. Chapter 2.

Activity 13-1: YEARLY FARM SCHEDULE (1880)

Skills. Summarizing written material in graphic form, skimming written material for specific information

Materials. Student copies of handout 13-1

Procedure

1. Introduce the lesson by reviewing the annual farm schedule of the nineteenth century. Work was seasonal and specific jobs were typically classified as men's work or women's work.

2. Distribute copies of handout 13-1. Encourage students to locate information in the chapter to complete the chart. Some work may only be implied in the chapter. For instance, if the chapter mentions that a garden is planted in the spring, the produce will be harvested in the summer and fall, even though the chapter may not specify harvesting garden products.

3. When students have had adequate time to complete the chart, share responses as a class. Contrast this pattern of living with ours today.

Name _____

	Spring	Summer	Fall	Winter
Work generally done by women				
Work generally done by men				

Directions. Use the information in the text to complete the chart.

Activity 13-2: PANORAMA OF IOWA FARMING

Skills. Summarizing written material in graphic form

Materials. Student copies of handouts 13-2a and 13-2b

Procedure

1. Introduce the lesson by reviewing the material in the chapter that relates to changes in Iowa's farm practices between 1880 and 1920. Students should recognize the technological advances had a profound effect on farm life between 1880 and 1920.

2. Distribute copies of handouts 13-2a and 13-2b. Using information discussed in class and material from the chapter, students will illustrate one aspect of farm life for the two periods. Space has been provided for students to write a descriptive statement for each illustration.

3. When the pictures are completed, provide space for students to display their work within the classroom.

Name _____

FARMING IN 1880-1900

_____

_____

_____

_____

_____

_____

_____

Name _____

FARMING IN 1900-1920

_____

_____

_____

_____

_____

_____

_____

Activity 13-3: HOUSEHOLD TASK COMPARISON

Skills. Completing a chart

Materials. Student copies of handout 13-3

Procedure

1. Discuss the fact that household tasks have traditionally been considered the domain of women. The following weekly schedule of jobs was almost universally accepted in the nineteenth and early twentieth centuries:

> Monday: Washing
> Tuesday: Ironing
> Wednesday: Sewing
> Thursday: Catching-up
> Friday: Cleaning
> Saturday: Baking
> Sunday: Resting

2. Distribute copies of handout 13-3. Have students complete the chart for their families.

3. When students have had adequate work time, discuss their responses, highlighting the differences between their weekly schedule and that of 1880.

In 1880 mother did the majority of the housework. Who does it today, and when is it done? Complete the following chart for your family.

1880		Who does this work today?	When is it done?
Monday	Washing		
Tuesday	Ironing		
Wednesday	Sewing		
Thursday	Catching-up		
Friday	Cleaning		
Saturday	Baking		
Sunday	Resting		

Activity 13-4: AGRICULTURAL EDUCATION PAST AND PRESENT

Skills. Completing a chart

Materials. Student copies of handout 13-4

Procedure

1. Introduce the lesson by reviewing the following means by which farmers in the early twentieth century (1910) learned about advancing technology and methodology related to agriculture:

   a. The extension service was just getting under way. Iowa State College provided farmers' institutes to disseminate the latest research on agricultural technology.
   b. Magazines like *Wallace's Farmer* were regularly read by Iowans.
   c. Newspapers often included columns with tips on agricultural practices.
   d. A select few Iowa farmers took advantage of the two-year agricultural course offered by Iowa State College in Ames.

2. Distribute copies of handout 13-4. Have students list ways in which farmers in 1910 learned about new methodology. Next have students list today's opportunities for agricultural education. By talking to friends, relatives, or classmates involved in agriculture, the following items may be identified:

   a. University programs with graduate and undergraduate courses in agriculture.
   b. Extension courses in each county.
   c. Numerous professional organizations, like the American Farm Bureau Federation, provide production and marketing information.
   d. Marketing trends can be monitored online.
   e. Computer-assisted management is available through software outlets and professional organizations.

3. Conclude the lesson by contrasting the availability of agricultural education opportunities in 1910 with today.

Name _____

AGRICULTURAL EDUCATION PAST AND PRESENT

Directions. In the left column list ways in which farmers in 1910 learned about methods of farming. In the right column list ways in which farmers today learn about new farming methods.

1910	Today

14 New Inventions Bring Change

CONTENT OBJECTIVES

Following the completion of the readings and activities for this chapter, students will have acquired the following understandings:

a. Technological advances of the 20th century had a profound impact on life in Iowa.
b. The telephone saved rural Iowans both time and money as cooperative companies were formed across the state.
c. The automobile, being fast and dependable, facilitated social and economic development as Iowans' individual mobility increased, allowing new businesses to flourish.
d. Electricity not only benefited agriculture and business but also provided many new time-saving conveniences for the home.

VOCABULARY TO KNOW

assembly line   kerosene

atomic power   livery stable

cooperative   switchboard

generators   tax

invention

PEOPLE TO IDENTIFY

Alexander Graham Bell   John Vincent Atanasoff

Frederick M. Hubbell   Thomas Edison

Henry Ford

FOR FURTHER STUDY

1. Take a tour of a local museum. Arrange for the tour guide to focus on the technological advances of the last century.

2. Tour the State Historical Museum in Des Moines. Many fine examples of technology from the past are a part of the collection.

REFERENCES

Bonney, Margaret, ed. "The Sky's the Limit." *The Goldfinch* 2, no.1 (September 1980). Iowa City: State Historical Society of Iowa.

_____,ed. "The Automobile Age." *The Goldfinch* 4, no.2. (November 1982). Iowa City: State Historical Society of Iowa.

Engle, Harry P., M.D. "The Most Satisfactory Investment for the Country Physician." *The Goldfinch,* Margaret Bonney, ed. 4, no.2 (November 1982). Reprinted from the *Journal of American Medical Association,* 1906. Iowa City: State Historical Society of Iowa.

Lovine, Marjorie. "A Kind of Human Machine: Woman's Work at the Switchboard." *The Palimpsest* 74, no. 1 (Spring 1993). Iowa City: State Historical Society of Iowa.

Nunnaly, Patrick. "From Churns to 'Butter Factories': The Industrialization of Iowa's Dairying, 1860-1900." *The Annals of Iowa* 49, no. 7 (Winter 1989). Iowa City: State Historical Society of Iowa.

Pittman, Von V., Jr. "Station WSUI and the Early Days of Instructional Radio." *The Palimpsest* 67, no.2 (March/April 1986). Iowa City: State Historical Society of Iowa.

Smith, Daniel Scott. "How a Half-Million Iowa Women Suddenly Went to Work—Solving a Mystery in the State Census of 1925." *The Annals of Iowa* 55, no. 4 (Fall 1996). Iowa City: State Historical Society of Iowa.

Swaim, Ginalie, ed. "Elevators and Ether, Weather Bureaus and Fountain Pens: 19th Century Bequests to the 20th." The *Iowa Heritage Illustrated* 80, no. 3 (Fall 1999). Iowa City: State Historical Society of Iowa.

Activity 14-1: DR. ENGLE'S NEW AUTOMOBILE

Skills. Reading and interpreting primary source material

Materials. Student copies of handout 14-1, Dr. Engle's testimonial (in text).

Procedure

1. Introduce the lesson by discussing the advantages of using the automobile.

2. Find the testimonial by Dr. Engle in the textbook. Distribute copies of handout 14-1. Read together the selection by Dr. Engle. Provide time for students to answer the questions related to the article.

3. Conclude the lesson by focusing on particular advantages of the automobile to Dr. Engle.

DR. ENGLE'S NEW AUTOMOBILE

Directions. Answer the following questions using the reading on Dr. Engle's automobile.

1. In what year was this article written? _____

2. Where did Dr. Engle live? _____

3. What did Dr. Engle use for transportation before he purchased his automobile?

_____

4. List and briefly describe at least four reasons why Dr. Engle found the automobile useful.

a. _____

b. _____

c. _____

d. _____

5. What problem with the automobile caused Dr. Engle the most concern?

_____

6. How did he plan to solve this problem?

_____

7. List other workers, besides doctors, who would have benefited from using an automobile.

_____   _____

_____   _____

_____   _____

Activity 14-2: THE AUTOMOBILE COMES TO IOWA

Skills. Collecting information from photographs

Materials. Study prints of early automobiles in text (motoring ladies, Oldsmobile in snow c. 1909, Ford Model T in mud, parade at Everly c. 1919), student copies of handout 14-2.

Procedure

1. Introduce the lesson by dividing the students into four small groups.
2. Assign to each group one of the four study prints. Have each group write a caption for the photograph and four observations about the use of the automobile based solely on the photograph.
3. After each group has completed its observations, take time for group reports.

THE AUTOMOBILE COMES TO IOWA

Directions. Using one of the study prints for this lesson, write a caption and list four observations about the automobile based on the photograph.

Caption: _____

_____

Observations:

a. _____

_____

b. _____

_____

c. _____

_____

d. _____

_____

Activity 14-3: INVENTIONS AND THEIR IMPACT ON IOWA

Skills. Making inferences based on content information

Materials. Transparency 14-3

Procedure

1. Introduce the lesson by having students name several inventions that made life easier for Iowans in the early part of the 20th century. Such items as the automobile, telephone, electricity, radio, etc., will be identified.

2. Project transparency 14-3. Have students suggest both positive and negative effects of each item, using the textbook as a source of information.

3. Conclude the lesson by discussing current technological advancement and potential hazards for today; i.e., nuclear power has both positive and negative potential.

INVENTIONS AND THEIR IMPACT ON IOWA

Invention	Positive Effects	Negative Effects
Automobile		
Telephone		
Electricity		
Gasoline tractor		
Airplane		
Television		
Phonograph		
Radio		

Activity 14-4: FIGURING TIME AND COST IN GRANDMA'S DAY

Skills. Reading road maps, using computational skills.

Materials. Student copies of handout 14-4, current road maps for pairs of students

Procedure

1. Introduce the lesson by discussing with students how automobile transportation has changed and continues to change. The cost of fuel and automobiles have changed over the years, as have speed limits, safety standards, etc.
2. Distribute copies of handout 14-4 and provide time for students to complete the computation.
3. Distribute current road maps. Have students perform the same computation using current data.
4. Conclude the lesson by comparing travel in 1937 with that of the present.

Name _____

FIGURING TIME AND COST IN GRANDMA'S DAY

Directions. Use the 1937 map insets to figure time and expense when traveling between Marshalltown and Des Moines.

Facts	Speed	35 miles per hour on pavement
		30 miles per hour on gravel
	Mileage	25 miles per gallon
	Cost	15 cents per gallon of gas

	Distance	Time	Cost
Marshalltown to Des Moines			
By way of Highways 30 and 65	_____	_____	_____
By way of Highways 14 and 6	_____	_____	_____
By way of Highways 88 and 30	_____	_____	_____

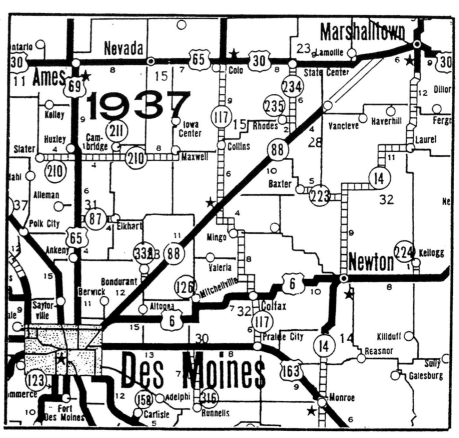

15 Business and Industry in Iowa

CONTENT OBJECTIVES

Following the completion of the readings and activities for this chapter, students will have acquired the following understandings:

a. Iowa's first industries, such as lumber milling, grain milling, and coal mining, depended on local natural resources.
b. The development of railroading was pivotal to the tremendous growth of Iowa industry after 1870.
c. Factory work opened new opportunities for Iowa women to work outside of the home.
d. As part of a global economy, Iowa's manufactured products are distributed throughout the nation and the world.

VOCABULARY TO KNOW

factory	manufacturing
household industry	millinery
industry	milling
lumbering	mining

PEOPLE TO IDENTIFY

John Boepple	John F. Hanson
Arthur Collins	Frederick Maytag
John Deere	Walter Sheaffer
George Douglas	John and Robert Stuart
Thomas Foster	

SOME IOWA INDUSTRIES

Amana Refrigeration, Inc.

Deere and Company

Featherlite Inc.

Fisher Controls International, Inc.

Lennox Industries Inc.

Maytag Corporation

Meredith Corporation

Pella Corporation

Pioneer Hi-Bred International, Inc.

Principal Financial Group

Quaker Oats Company

Rockwell Avionics and Communications

Winnebago Industries, Inc.

FOR FURTHER STUDY

1. Visit a local industry. Find out how it got started, what it produces, where products are shipped, and how many people are employed.

2. Discuss what might be potential industries of the future. What place might Iowa play in the development of future industrial endeavor?

3. Write to your local representative to Congress and find out what is being done to encourage new industries in Iowa.

REFERENCE

Bonney, Margaret, ed. "Early Manufacturing." *The Goldfinch* 2, no.2 (November 1980). Iowa City: State Historical Society of Iowa.

_____ed. "The Town Builders of Iowa." *The Goldfinch* 3, no.3 (February 1982). Iowa City: State Historical Society of Iowa.

Farley, Mary Allison. "Iowa Women in the Workplace." *The Palimpsest* 67, no.1 (January/February 1986). Iowa City: State Historical Society of Iowa.

Fink, Deborah. *Cutting into the Meatpacking Line: Workers and Change in the Rural Midwest.* Chapel Hill: University of North Carolina Press, 1998.

Friedricks, William B. "The Newspaper That Captured a State: A History of the *Des Moines Register* 1849-1985." *The Annals of Iowa* 54, no. 4 (Fall 1995). Iowa City: State Historical Society of Iowa.

Gradwohl, David M., and Nancy M. Osborn. *Exploring Buried Buxton.* Ames: Iowa State University Press, 1984.

Mutel, Cornalie. "Water Powered Mills in Iowa: A Foresaken Technology." *The Palimpsest* 77, no. 4 (Winter 1996). Iowa City: State Historical Society of Iowa.

Schwieder, Dorothy. "Economic Development: Iowa's Industries and Industrial Workers." In *Iowa: The Middle Land.*" Iowa State University Press, 1996. Chapter 2.

Warren, Wilson J. "The Welfare Capitalism of John Morrell and Company, 1922-1937." *The Annals of Iowa* 47, no.6 (Fall 1984). Iowa City: State Historical Society of Iowa.

Activity 15-1: EARLY IOWA INDUSTRY

Skills. Reading a chart

Materials. United States wall map, transparency 15-1 (also in text), six study prints of lumber industry (in text)

Procedure

1. Introduce the lesson by reviewing the material in the text related to Iowa's early industries. Between 1833 and 1870 industries gradually developed to meet the economic demands of the settlers who bought land and settled in Iowa. After 1870 the railroad spanned the state, making it possible to transport goods more quickly. As a result, Iowa became tied to the national economy in ways which were never before possible.

2. Project transparency 15-1 or locate chart in textbook. Provide time for students to observe the data on this chart. Discuss the top five industries for each year, drawing possible conclusions as to why some industries maintained their importance and others did not.

3. Direct students' attention to the lumber industry. Note that lumber was one of the leading industries from 1870 to 1910. By 1910 the pineries of northern Minnesota and Wisconsin had been exhausted. Have students suggest possible interpretations for the data on this table, noting that more data would be needed in order to conclusively depict Iowa's lumber industry relative to Iowa's total industrial growth.

4. Using a map of the United States, briefly review the following facts about the lumber industry, noting Iowa's relationship to the nation:

   a. Most of the lumber for Iowa's sawmills came from the forests of Wisconsin and Minnesota.
   b. Logs were rafted down the Mississippi.
   c. Companies in Iowa's Mississippi river towns purchased the raw material.
   d. Logs were processed into finished products.
   e. Finished products were shipped to distributors and retailers across the country.

5. Have students retell the story of Iowa's early lumber industry by examining the six study prints in proper sequence.

THE FIVE LEADING IOWA MANUFACTURING AND PROCESSING INDUSTRIES BY YEAR

Industry	Census Year							
	1870	1880	1890	1900	1910	1920	1930	1940
Flour and gristmill products	X	X	X	X				
Lumber	X	X	X	X	X			
Furniture	X							
Meat packing		X	X	X	X	X	X	X
Carpentering and building	X		X	X				
Woolen goods	X							
Carriages and wagons		X						
Blacksmithing		X						
Printing and publishing			X		X	X	X	X
Railroad cars, repairs, etc.			X	X	X	X		
Foundry and machine shop products					X	X	X	
Food preparations						X		
Household appliances							X	
Bread and bakery products							X	X
Corn syrup, sugar, oil, etc.								X
Planing mills not with sawmills								X

Activity 15-2: IOWA PRODUCTS DAY

Skills. Identifying specific locations using maps, creating a classroom display

Materials. Pamphlets on Iowa industries, magazines containing product advertisements, Iowa wall map, art materials for creating displays

Procedure

1. Introduce the lesson by reviewing the names of Iowa industries manufacturing consumer products. Companies such as Maytag, Amana, Deere & Company and Quaker Oats would logically be suggested.

2. Plan an Iowa products day for the classroom. Encourage students to locate products or advertisements for products manufactured in Iowa. Students will create displays highlighting specific companies. Included might be ads, promotional pamphlets, and actual products.

3. A large classroom map should be displayed, identifying locations of the Iowa industries being highlighted.

4. Invite other classes to visit the room to view the displays.

For information on Iowa business, contact the Department of Economic Development, 200 E. Grand, Des Moines, Iowa 50309.

Activity 15-3: LOCAL INDUSTRY

Skills. Taking a survey, creating a bar graph

Materials. Large poster paper for making the bar graph

Procedure

1. Introduce the lesson by reviewing the information gained on Iowa industry, i.e., Iowa has several corporations which manufacture products for state, national, and international markets.

2. Have students identify the major industries in the community or nearby communities. After a list has been generated, assign specific industries to either individuals or committees of students. The industries should be surveyed, with students collecting information on the number of workers currently being employed.

3. After the information has been collected, a bar graph could be made by the class illustrating the number of workers employed by each local industry. Discuss the relative importance of each industry to the local economy.

Activity 15-4: CURRENT IOWA INDUSTRIES

Skills. Letter writing

Materials. Iowa wall map

Procedure

1. Introduce the lesson by having the students identify as many Iowa industries as they can. Predictably, Deere & Company, Maytag, Amana, and Quaker Oats will be mentioned.

2. Next have students suggest possible ways to further investigate Iowa industry. The Department of Economic Development will provide pamphlets highlighting Iowa's industries. Students could request information on Iowa industry by writing to: The Iowa Department of Economic Development, 200 E. Grand Ave., Des Moines, IA 50309.

3. When this information has been collected, students could contact specific industries and request promotional information. Encourage students to focus on types of products, as well as markets for these products. Many Iowa industries distribute nationally and internationally.

4. To provide a focus for this investigation, display a large classroom map of Iowa. As information is collected materials could be displayed on the map.

Note: This activity requires several weeks to complete.

Activity 15-5: MINING COUNTY BY COUNTY

Skills. Using reference books, preparing written summaries

Materials. Reference books on mining, writing materials

Procedure

1. Introduce the lesson by focusing on Iowa's historic coal mining industry. Review the information covered in the chapter relating to coal mining.

2. Suggest to students that every county in Iowa has some form of mining. Students generally associate mining with the traditional shaft mine operation when in fact any extraction of minerals from the earth is a form of mining.

3. Have students suggest types of mining in Iowa other than coal mining. Over half of Iowa's counties produce limestone. Eighty percent of the counties produce sand and gravel. In addition, clay, shale, and gypsum are major products.

4. Have students research to find out what minerals are mined in their county. They may wish to contact the Chamber of Commerce, consult a reference librarian, and discuss the matter with their parents.

5. After the county's mining operations have been identified, have students locate the sites and write a brief description of the mining process. Possibly a worker could be interviewed and a recording of the interview shared with the class. In addition, students may wish to take pictures of the mining site to share with the class.

16 World War I and Hard Times After

CONTENT OBJECTIVES

Following the completion of the readings and activities for this chapter, students will have acquired the following understandings:

a. In the early years of WW I, Americans attempted to be neutral and avoid entering the war.
b. On April 6, 1917, America entered WWI by declaring war on Germany.
c. Iowans participated in the war by sending soldiers, purchasing war bonds, and producing large amounts of agricultural products. Women played important new roles.
d. On the Iowa home front, anti-German sentiment was rampant. Many people thought it was patriotic to remove any suggestion of German culture.

VOCABULARY TO KNOW

armistice

blockade

depression, The Great Depression

fundamental

interest

military draft

neutral

rationing

submarine

PEOPLE TO IDENTIFY

Franklin Roosevelt

Henry A. Wallace

Herbert Hoover

Merle Hay

Woodrow Wilson

FOR FURTHER STUDY

1. Have students consult the local historical society for artifacts from the World War I era.

2. Invite a senior citizen to class who farmed during the Depression. Have students prepare to discuss changes in Iowa's farm practices and opportunities.

3. Encourage students to make maps showing those countries involved in World War I.

REFERENCES

Behrens, Roy R. "Iowa's Contribution to Camouflage." *The Palimpsest* 78, no. 3 (Fall 1997). Iowa City: State Historical Society of Iowa.

Carter, Merle Wright, and Dean Gabbert. "Hospital Unit R in World War I: Fairfield to France." *The Palimpsest* 67, no.5 (September/October 1986). Iowa City: State Historical Society of Iowa.

Derr, Nancy. "Lowden: A Study of Intolerance in an Iowa Community During the Era of the First World War." *The Annals of Iowa* 50, no. 1 (Summer 1989). Iowa City: State Historical Society of Iowa.

Grant, H. Roger, and L. Edward Purcell, eds. *Years of Struggle: The Fann Diary of Elmer G. Powers, 1931-1936.* Ames: Iowa State University Press, 1976.

Morain, Tom. *Prairie Grass Roots: An Iowa Small Town in the Early Twentieth Century.* Ames: Iowa State University Press, 1988.

Plambeck, Herb. "The National Drought Conference in Des Moines: When FDR and Alf Landon Met." *The Palimpsest* 67, no.6 (November/December 1986). Iowa City: State Historical Society of Iowa.

Ryan, Thomas G. "Supporters and Opponents of Prohibition: Iowa in 1917." *The Annals of Iowa* 46, no.7 (Winter 1983). Iowa City: State Historical Society of Iowa.

Swaim, Ginalie, ed. "Hard Times in Iowa, 1920s and 1930s." *The Goldfinch* 7, no.4 (April 1986). Iowa City: State Historical Society of Iowa.

————, ed. "Public and Private Words from Unit R." *The Palimpsest* 67, no. 5 (September, October 1986). Iowa City: State Historical Society of Iowa.

Activity 16-1: EFFECTS OF THE WAR

Skills. Skimming written material for specific information

Materials. Student copies of handout 16-1

Procedure

1. Begin the lesson by reviewing the text material related to the contributions Iowans made to the war effort. Discuss several ways Iowans helped with the war effort.

2. Distribute copies of handout 16-1. Encourage students to identify the effects or outcomes of these war efforts. For example, many Iowans were drafted into military service, and as a result, many were killed in Europe.

3. When students have completed handout 16-1, discuss their responses, emphasizing the short- and long-term effects of the war on society, politics, and the economy.

Name _____

EFFECTS OF THE WAR

Directions. Identify three ways Iowans contributed to World War I. List the effect each contribution had in the column on the right.

Contribution to the War	Effect

1. _____   _____

   _____   _____

   _____   _____

   _____   _____

2. _____   _____

   _____   _____

   _____   _____

   _____   _____

3. _____   _____

   _____   _____

   _____   _____

   _____   _____

Activity 16-2: FARM DIARY OF ELMER POWERS

Skills. Reading and interpreting primary source materials

Materials. Powers's farm diary (in text)

Procedure

1. Introduce the lesson by reviewing with students the textbook material related to the agricultural depression following World War I.

2. Find the pages of Powers's diary. Note that Elmer Powers was farming during the 1930s when the Great Depression was at its lowest point.

3. After reading and discussing the selection, conclude the lesson by discussing the following questions:

   a. In what ways was life on the farm different from that of people in cities during the Depression? See May 20, 1931, and June 2, 1931.

   b. What was Mr. Powers's attitude toward hard times? See act. 23, 1935; Jan. 6 and 14, 1936; act. 1, 1936; Dec. 31, 1936.

   c. Farmers had a hard time during the Depression. Find an entry in each year that describes the problems farmers faced.

Activity 16-3: THE COST OF LIVING, 1934-1936

Skills. Comparing and contrasting current data with that of an earlier period

Materials. Cost of living table (in text)

Procedure

1. Begin the lesson by locating the cost of living table in text. Ask students to compare the cost of items in 1934 with those today. Predictably, many students will notice the low prices for items without noticing the low salaries.

2. Discuss the following questions:

   a. If a depression happened in the next year, which of these items would show a decline in sales? Why?

bread	televisions	meat
shoes	campers	woolen mittens
boats	candy	pop

   b. What effect would a decline in sales have on employment?

   c. Think about someone you know who has a job. Would a decline in sales affect that person's job?

   d. Think about the salaries and costs of living today. Compare them with Depression figures. Has everything gone up in the same proportion?

1931

May 20-Wednesday. These farm folks in this county are doing quite well in adjusting themselves to the existing times. Driving along the highway, I picked up a young man who said that he was from the east. He described conditions there, as he sees them, and talked about the bitterness of many of those people. He asked about people here and I told him that folks here always have something to eat and also always have our minds and hands busy. Two things that help much to keep people contented.

June 2-Tuesday. Worked in corn stalk ground, spring plowed. Plenty of trouble with stalks and lots of hard work to do good cultivating. But not a bad job at that. There wasn't any foreman who had to be pleased or to find fault with my work. I know I can still work here tomorrow. The place won't be shut down.

1932

June 13-Monday. Drove to town with the truck, marketing hogs. We were paid $2.25 per cwt., much the lowest price we ever received for hogs. Five years ago today they were $6.50.

July 21-Thursday. Our daily paper has stopped and we are not renewing it now. As a matter of economy I am resharpening old razor blades and when I shave I use any kind of soap instead of shaving cream. The oats market is a cent lower today.

September 19-Monday. Everyone is trading now. I did a little today myself, trading sorghum for grapes. As a matter of economy I shaved today with a dime store blade. But it is the farm women who think out and do things to save money.

October 14-Friday. Conditions in some places are very bad. Some farmers do not seem to have any intentions of husking their corn. Many folks intend to use some corn for fuel. One court house is being heated with corn.

December 25-Sunday. Our family enjoyed a Christmas Dinner with the old folks at their home in the village. No gifts were exchanged by the grown folks. However, the smaller children were well remembered.

1933

Throughout the year of 1933 conditions did not improve. Toward the end of the year Mr. Powers wrote that he "could see great need for instant action in aiding agriculture."

1934

January 11-Thursday. "No we don't get the paper anymore," is a statement I hear quite frequently. Earl May and his station seem to be the most dependable source of information.

May 23-Wednesday. I spent the forenoon rebuilding an old cultivator. Buying a new one is out of the question. With these crop prospects anyway.

June 4-Monday. We were behind a month on our phone rent and the linemen disconnected it today. Perhaps many farm folks will do without many things soon.

June 30-Saturday. This afternoon I attended a dispersal sale of a Holstein herd. A neighbor is working thru the system of "going bankrupt" and the sale is one of the results.

November 12-Monday. Al came to husk this morning and we finished the job at noon. Of all the crops I have gathered, this is the poorest one. Our cribs are almost empty and almost all of the feeding season is before us. Now I, like many others must sell or almost give away hogs because I cannot feed them or buy feed for them.

November 24-Saturday. Of the very many Thanksgivings I can remember, this one is an outstanding one in the few things that we think we have to be thankful for.

1935

February 16-Saturday. Tonight we went back to our old custom of driving in to the county seat for the evening. We had not been to town on Saturday night for some time. I went to the implement store and found prices of many articles too high. At least I cannot buy them and pay for them.

April 19-Monday. We stopped at the cold storage plant and learned about the new plan of storing our fresh killed meat in our own rented locker. Where it is kept at zero or the proper temperature for storage. We plan to use this service. It will cost a dollar a month, or nine dollars per year.

July 9-Thursday. The earth is dry and hard and many large cracks are appearing in the stubble field. Any tools that I carry on the binder may be dropped down in these cracks. I tied a string on the handle of a 12 in. crescent wrench and lowered it down a crack. I will not mention the distance. Some things are better left unsaid. ...

October 23-Wednesday. Today two farm ladies were discussing the problem of how best to remove the printed letters from seed sacks that they wished to use in some of their sewing work. On many farms feed sacks are made up into various useful things by the very resourceful farm women.

December 4-Wednesday. I went to town this morning to see the bankers. I will have to sell grain and livestock to pay the mortgage holder, so that I can get the Federal Loan.

1936

January 6-Monday. We had another winter day again and here at the place we sold the baler. In some ways I regret to see it go. The money I received for it will be very useful just now in closing up the loan affairs.

January 14-Tuesday. I think I finished the loan business today. I got the Federal Land Bank money and it was sent to pay off the old mortgage. All of the people connected with this problem have been very nice. Tomorrow I think I can begin to plan for a new future.

January 22-Wednesday. School attendance was as low as the thermometer. Many schools were closed. No mail anywhere today. The bitter cold was very bad for all livestock. Our stock suffered some and they consumed large amounts of feed.

April 24-Friday. We began spring plowing today. We will use both the tractor and the horse plows. A good rain is much needed by all growing things.

June 27-Saturday. The heat in our corn fields today was very intense. The pastures are rapidly turning a deep burned brown in color.

July 5-Sunday. Late this afternoon I borrowed enough iron pipe to reach from the windmill pump to our garden and will pump water on the garden all night. We do not expect to be able to water all of the garden, but may save some of it. The vegetables that will be most useful for canning purposes.

July 19-Sunday. The greatest corn crop disaster that our country has ever experienced is upon us. It may take some little time for all people to realize this, but all will know as time goes on.

September 15-Tuesday. Today was a rainy day, all day. It is the first rainy day for months. It was interesting to watch the livestock and the poultry. The younger ones did not seem to know just what the rain was.

October 1-Thursday. Since our pastures are becoming green again I have been thinking that we should have more young cattle in them. I drove to see the banker and he favored the idea. He suggested that I go out and buy whatever I wanted and come in and we would fix up a loan to cover the purchases.

October 2-Friday. I drove over to a neighbors this morning and bot a white face calf from him, paying ten dollars for it. I went to another community sale and bot five more calves. I paid $49.50 for these.

December 31-Thursday. I have written 1936 for the last time and tomorrow a New Year begins. I am facing it knowing there are hardships in the future for farm folks and I hope there will not be too many for us all.

FROM: *Years of Struggle: The Farm Diary of Elmer G. Powers, 1931-1936,* H. Roger Grant and L. Edward Purcell, eds. Iowa State University Press, Ames, Iowa. 1976.

17 Depression, Changing Times, and World War II

CONTENT OBJECTIVES

Following the completion of the readings and activities for this chapter, students will have acquired the following understandings:

a. Following WW I, farm prices steadily fell, causing economic depression and hardship for many Iowans.
b. Because of high unemployment during the 1930s, the federal government responded with work programs that not only provided jobs but also developed Iowa's roads, parks, and public buildings.
c. Despite the economic hardships, many technological advancements occurred during the Depression, making motion pictures, radio, and automobiles accessible to more people.
d. Both men and women took on new roles after WW II.
e. Iowans felt the impact of events around the world as the state emerged from the Depression, entered the WW II era, and moved into the atomic age.

VOCABULARY TO KNOW

atomic bomb	Nagasaki
bootleggers	Pearl Harbor
Civilian Conservation Corps (CCC)	Prohibition
Far East	Soviet Union
Hiroshima	"talkies"
Ku Klux Klan	Works Progress Administration (WPA)

PEOPLE TO IDENTIFY

Billy Robinson	Orville and Wilbur Wright
Colonel B. J. Palmer	

FOR FURTHER STUDY

1. Invite a panel of Iowa World War II veterans to class and have them describe their experiences to the students. Class members should prepare questions for the panel discussion and, if possible, submit them to panel members prior to the visit.

2. Have selected students investigate the history of the battleship Iowa, which has recently been recommissioned by the United States Navy. Students should report the results of their research to the entire class.

3. Assign students to make brief reports on how technological changes that took place in the 1930s influenced the American way of life. Students should also include businesses that have grown because of these changes.

4. Have students prepare a large chart that includes statistics about America 1950. The chart might contain population density, urban-rural ratios, cost of selected items, number of states, and other appropriate information.

5. The teacher should investigate any local construction projects that took place under the auspices of the WPA or the CCC. In Iowa, WPA workers built roads, dams, parks, and public buildings, and the CCC planted forests and built artificial lakes. See if students can make any generalizations about the types of work completed and/or architectural designs, etc. In your community look for sidewalks, bridges, parks, tennis courts, gymnasiums, stadiums, schools, fairgrounds, town halls, stone gates at park entrances, and murals. These are often marked with plaques.

REFERENCES

Andrews, Clarance. "Sheldon, Iowa During WWII." *The Palimpsest* 70, no. 3 (Fall 1989). Iowa City: State Historical Society of Iowa.

Bauer, Patrick. "Farm Mortgage Relief Legislation in Iowa During the Great Depression." *The Annals of Iowa* 50, no. 1 (Summer 1989). Iowa City: State Historical Society of Iowa.

"Beuscher Family Interview" by Jessie A. Bloodworth and Elizabeth J. Greenwood under the supervision of John N. Webb, Coordinator of Urban Research, Works Progress Administration. In *The Personal* Side, 1939. Reprint edition, 1971, Arno Press, Inc. and Explorations in Iowa History Project. Cedar Falls, Malcolm Price Laboratory School, University of Northern Iowa.

Bonney, Margaret, ed. "War!" *The Goldfinch* 4, no. 4 (April 1983). Iowa City: State Historical Society Iowa.

"The Depression and After," *The Palimpsest* 63, no. 1 (January/February 1982). Iowa City: State Historical Society of Iowa.

Fish, Donald. "Remembrances of a County Agricultural Agent in the Great Depression." *The Palimpsest* 72, no. 2 (Summer 1991). Iowa City: State Historical Society of Iowa.

"The Great Depression." *The Goldfinch* (Fall 1978). Iowa City: State Historical Society of Iowa.

Jellison, Katherine. "'Let Your Corn Stalks Buy a Maytag:' Prescriptive Literature and Domestic Consumerism in Rural Iowa, 1929-1939." *The Palimpsest* 69, no. 3 (Fall 1988) Iowa City: State Historical Society of Iowa.

Martin, Dorris B. "A Congressional Wife in Wartime Washington." *The Palimpsest* 64, no. 2 (March/April 1983). Iowa City: State Historical Society of Iowa.

Meusburger, Joanne. "Farm Girl." *The Palimpsest* 68, no. 4 (Winter 1987). Iowa City: State Historical Society of Iowa.

Narber, Gregg R., and Lea Rosson DeLong. "The New Deal Murals in Iowa." *The Palimpsest* 63, no. 3 (May /June 1982). Iowa City: State Historical Society of Iowa.

Regan, Stephen D. " 'The Mighty I': The USS Iowa Story." *The Palimpsest* 64, no. 2 (March/April 1983) Iowa City: State Historical Society of Iowa.

Saloutos, Theodore, and John D. Hicks. "The Farm Strike." In *Patterns and Perspectives in Iowa History*. Dorothy Schwieder, ed. Ames: Iowa State University Press, 1973.

Salvaneschi, Lenore. "Fuel." *The Palimpsest* 66, no.6 (November/December 1985). Iowa City: State Historical Society of Iowa.

Schwieder, Dorothy. "The 1930's: A Time of Trial." In *Iowa: The Middle Land.* Iowa State University Press, 1996. Chapter 3.

"Some Thoughts on Prisoners of War in Iowa, 1943 to 1946," *The Palimpsest* 65, no.2 (March/April 1984) Iowa City: State Historical Society of Iowa.

Activity 17-1: THE BEUSCHER FAMILY OF DUBUQUE

Skills. Reading and interpreting primary source materials

Materials. Student copies of handout 17-1, the Beuscher family interview (in text)

Procedure

1. Introduce the lesson by reviewing the material from the text related to the Depression and its effect on Iowans.

2. Find the Beuscher interview in the text and read the introduction together. Provide time for students to read the selection and answer the questions.

3. When students have completed the reading and have answered the questions, discuss the Depression experience from the point of view of the Beuscher family.

4. Use this discussion to encourage students to go into the community and interview a person who remembers the Depression in Iowa. Have students share their findings with the class.

　　　　　　　　　Name _____

THE BEUSCHER FAMILY OF DUBUQUE

      Mr. Beuscher has only one suggested solution for the problem of unemployment: persons of "wealth" should be persuaded to invest their money in industries that might increase or create new employment. He believes also that there should be a better "distribution" of the money paid for commodities. But Mr. Beuscher does not hold "radical" ideas. At one time there was quite a group of Socialists in Dubuque; now the movement has "died out."

1. What different jobs did Mr. Beuscher have? _____

_____

2. How did both Mr. and Mrs. Beuscher help to provide for the family? _____

_____

_____

_____

_____

3. How did the Beuscher family feel about receiving aid from the government? _____

_____

_____

_____

Activity 17-2: WET VERSUS DRY

Skills. Formulating opinions and discussing controversial issues

Materials. Student copies of handout 17-2

Procedure

1. Introduce the lesson by reviewing the text material related to Prohibition. Discuss the concept of constitutional amendment.
2. Distribute copies of handout 17-2. Read the directions together and provide time for students to answer the questions.
3. Conclude the lesson by discussing this issue from today's perspective.

WET VERSUS DRY

Directions.

    Read the two constitutional amendments below and answer the questions which follow, using your textbook and other resource material.

    18TH AMENDMENT: *Prohibition of Intoxicating Liquors*
    SECTION 1. After one year from the ratification of this article the manufacture, sale or transportation of intoxicating liquors within the importation thereof into, or the exportation thereof from the United States and all territory subject to the jurisdiction thereof for beverage purposes is hereby prohibited.
    SECTION 2. The Congress and the several States shall have concurrent power to enforce this article by appropriate legislation.
    SECTION 3. This article shall be inoperative unless it shall have been ratified as an amendment to the Constitution by the legislatures of the several States, as provided in the Constitution, within seven years of the date of the submission hereof to the States by Congress.

    [Proposed Dec. 18, 1917; ratified Jan. 16, 1919.]

    21ST AMENDMENT: *Repeal of 18th Amendment*
    SECTION 1. The Eighteenth article of amendment to the Constitution of the United States is hereby repealed.
    SECTION 2. The transportation or importation into any State, Territory, or possession of the United States for delivery or use therein of intoxicating liquors, in violation of the laws thereof, is hereby prohibited.
    SECTION 3. This article shall be inoperative unless it shall have been ratified as an amendment to the Constitution by conventions in the several States, as provided in the constitution, within seven years from the date of the submission hereof to the States by the Congress.

    [Proposed Feb. 20, 1933; ratified Dec. 5, 1933.]

1. How long did it take before the Eighteenth Amendment was repealed?_____

_____

2. Why did Prohibition fail? _____

_____

_____

3. List and explain at least three laws that you feel are unpopular today.

_____

_____

_____

_____

_____

_____

_____

4. What kind of laws control the sale and use of alcohol today? What group of people is responsible for passing these laws? Enforcing them?

_____

_____

_____

_____

_____

_____

Activity 17-3: FROM NEW YORK TO PARIS

Skills. Producing facsimiles of primary source documents

Materials. Art materials for making posters

Procedure

1. Introduce the lesson by reviewing the text material related to the early use of the airplane in Iowa.
2. Provide students with the following information:

In 1919 a New York hotel owner named Raymond Orteig offered a $25,000 prize for the first person to fly nonstop from New York to Paris. Charles Lindbergh made the flight on May 20 and 21, 1927, and won the prize money.

3. Have students design and construct posters advertising this award to aviators. Students will need to have the following information:

Reward: $25,000
For: First nonstop flight from New York to Paris (3600 miles)
Offered by: Raymond Orteig of New York
When: 1919
Why: Adventure, and promotion of advances in aviation

4. Conclude the lesson by discussing present-day counterparts of the early aviation experiments.

PRIMARY SOURCE MATERIAL: The Beuscher Family Interview (unabridged)

This is a summary of an interview which was completed December 13, 1937 as a WPA project.

Mr. Beuscher, 62 years old, had been working for 29 years for the Dubuque railroad shops when they closed in 1931. He was recalled to work at the shops after he had been unemployed for 4 years. Tall, gangling, weather-beaten, he stoops forward when he talks so that he may follow the conversation with greater ease, for he is more than a little deaf.

Mrs. Beuscher is 2 years younger than her husband. She is the mother of 11 children, but has found time to make dresses and coats and suits, not only for her own family, but also for customers outside the home.

As they "look back on it," Mr. and Mrs. Beuscher scarcely know how they did manage to get along during the time that he had no regular work. The irregular income from Mrs. Beuscher's sewing continued, though she was forced to lower prices until earnings averaged no more than $3 or $4 a week. For a year after Mr. Beuscher lost his job [in 1931], the family's only cash income was the four hundred seventy-odd dollars obtained from the insurance policies and Mrs. Beuscher's irregular earnings, as contrasted with the predepression regular income of about $130 a month, Mr. Beuscher's full-time earnings.

Mr. and Mrs. Beuscher agreed that application for relief was a virtual necessity. Mr. Beuscher remembers going down to the courthouse for the first time as the hardest thing he ever had to do in his life; his hand was "on the door-knob five times" before he turned it. The investigation, which the Beuschers recognized as necessary and inevitable, was so prolonged that Mrs. Beuscher "really didn't think" that the family would ever get relief. But finally, after about 2 months, a grocery order of $4.50 was granted. Mrs. Beuscher had long before learned to "manage" excellently on little, and though the order was meager, the family "got along" and "always had enough to eat." Mrs. Beuscher believes that investigators "did the best they could;" she resents only their insistence on the disconnection of the telephone, on which she depended for keeping in touch with her customers.

Soon Mr. Beuscher was assigned as a laborer to county relief work, for which he was paid, always in grocery orders, $7.20 a week; this increased amount gave the family a little more leeway. Yet they were still without much cash. The family's garden, for which the city furnished some of the seeds and the plot of ground on the city island, added fresh vegetables to the list of staples which alone could be purchased on the grocery orders; there were even some vegetables to be sold from house to house, and Mrs. Beuscher canned a little almost every day, just as the vegetables were ready for use. One summer she put up 500 quarts of vegetables.

Although the Beuschers never felt comfortable about receiving relief, it came to be more or less an accepted thing. "You know, you went down to City Hall, and had to wait in line, and you saw all your friends; it was funny in a way, though it was pitiful, too. ... People went down to the relief office, and talked about going, just the way they might have gone anywhere else."

The family received food orders for only a few months, as Mr. Beuscher was soon assigned to the CWA Eagle Point Park project as a laborer, earning 40¢ an hour. Later he worked on the lock and dam project at 50¢ an hour. Mr. Beuscher cannot understand why there was so great a difference between the wage rates of laborers on work projects and those of skilled carpenters. Although he was glad to be assigned to projects, there was little essential difference in his feelings about direct relief and about "work relief'; he worked hard for his pay, but still felt that he was being "given something." He has heard many times that persons on relief do not want work and will not accept jobs in private industry, but he knows from project employees whose reactions were similar to his that such is not the case, except perhaps in a very few instances.

Although Mr. and Mrs. Beuscher "don't say the depression is over yet," times have been better for them since the late fall of 1935, when Mr. Beuscher was called back to his old work at the shops at the old rate of pay. Mr. Beuscher considers this "regular work," and, as such, far superior to relief work, especially as he now "feels more independent." Still, it is not as it was in the old days when 1,500 men were employed rebuilding damaged and out-worn cars. Of the 130 men taken back at the shop, only 25 remain at work, which now consists of wrecking instead of reclamation, and no one of the 25 men knows how long his work will last.

Mr. Beuscher has only one suggested solution for the problem of unemployment: persons of "wealth" should be persuaded to invest their money in industries that might increase or create new employment. He believes also that there should be a better "distribution" of the money paid for commodities. But Mr. Beuscher does not hold "radical" ideas. At one time there was quite a group of Socialists in Dubuque; now the movement has "died out."

FROM: *The Personal Side.* 1939. Reprinted 1971. Jessie A. Bloodworth and Elizabeth J. Greenwood, eds. New York: Arno Press.

18 The Story Continues

CONTENT OBJECTIVES

Following the completion of the readings and activities for this chapter, students will have acquired the following understandings:

a. Declining population in rural areas has had a major impact on rural communities, schools systems, and politics.
b. Iowa, having some of the richest soil in the world, produces surplus agricultural products.
c. The practice of soil conservation helps to protect Iowa's rich soil.
d. While Iowa has traditionally been a heavily Republican state, today both the Republican and Democratic parties are strong.
e. Iowans have pioneered in the development of new agriculture processes, computers, and the exploration of outer space.
f. Iowans today are part of a world community.

VOCABULARY TO KNOW

consolidation   soil bank, soil conservation

population   vocation

PEOPLE TO IDENTIFY

Dr. Norman Borlaug   Dr. James Van Allen

FOR FURTHER STUDY

1. Have representatives from the class consult the Department of Natural Resources or your county conservation board to obtain information on the current status of conservation efforts in Iowa. Free materials are available which will be helpful and interesting for students.

2. Have students make a map showing where Iowa's colleges and universities are

located. The map could be color-coded to designate colleges, universities, state schools, private schools, and area community colleges.

REFERENCES

Boyle, Matthew. "Serving the Cause of Peace: The Iowa Campuses' Vietnam Protest." *The Palimpsest* 63, no. 5(September/October 1982). Iowa City: State Historical Society of Iowa.

Field, Bruce. "The Price of Dissent: The Iowa Farmers Union and the Early Cold War, 1945-1954." *The Annals of Iowa* 55, no. 1 (Winter 1996). Iowa City: State Historical Society of Iowa.

Hawbaker, Becky Wilson. "Early Television for Iowa's Children." *The Palimpsest* 75, no. 2 (Summer 1994). Iowa City: State Historical Society of Iowa.

Schwieder, Dorothy. "Iowa in the Sixties and Seventies." In *Iowa: The Middle Land.* Iowa State University Press, 1996. Chapter 3.

Schwieder, Dorothy. "Iowa: The 1980's and 1990's." In *Iowa: The Middle Land.* Iowa State University Press, 1996. Chapter 3.

Smith, Thomas S. "The Vietnam Era in Iowa Politics." *The Palimpsest* 63, no.5 (September/October 1982). Iowa City: State Historical Society of Iowa.

Warren, Wilson *I.* "'The People's Century' in Iowa: Coalition-Building Among Farm and Labor Organizations, 1945-1950." *The Palimpsest* 49, no.5 (Summer 1988). Iowa City: State Historical Society of Iowa.

Activity 18-1: SCHOOL CONSOLIDATION

Skills. Using local resources

Materials. Local historical resources

Procedure

1. Review the fact that when Iowa was originally surveyed and divided into townships and sections, section 16 in each township was reserved for education. This land was usually sold or rented to provide revenue for schools of the township. From Iowa's early years until the middle of the twentieth century, the countryside was dotted with one-room schools. By 1960 most of these schools in Iowa had been closed as the need for school consolidations increased.

2. By consulting the local library, city offices, historical society, or senior citizens, have students investigate where the original schools were located in and around their community. Individual reports could include interview summaries, copies of photographs and documents, and artifacts from school days long ago.

3. Provide space in the room to display student work and allow time for students to share their findings with classmates.

Activity 18-2: GLOBAL INTERDEPENDENCE

Skills. Creating a graph

Materials. Student copies of handout 18-2, chart paper

Procedure

1. Introduce the lesson by discussing global interdependence and the importance of this concept in the modern world. Relate this discussion to Iowa's place in the world and the influence of other parts of the world on Iowa.

2. Distribute copies of handout 18-2. Have students complete the questions for their families.

3. When the questions have been completed, have students use chart paper to create a classroom graph illustrating the results of the questionnaire.

4. Conclude the lesson by contrasting self-sufficient pioneer Iowa with interdependent modern Iowa. (Example: Pioneer Iowans raised or made most of their own food, clothing, and shelter. Twentieth-century Iowans heat their homes with natural gas from the Southwest, wear clothing produced overseas or in the East, eat foods produced in many parts of the country, drive cars made in the United States, Europe, or Japan, and travel to almost every corner of the earth.)

GLOBAL INTERDEPENDENCE

Directions. Mark each statement below which is true for you or anyone in your family.

1. _____ Owns toys from another country.

2. _____ Collects foreign stamps.

3. _____ Has eaten in a restaurant specializing in foreign food.

4. _____ Eats or drinks imported foods, such as coffee, chocolate, tea, bananas.

5. _____ Has hosted someone from another country.

6. _____ Owns clothing imported from another country.

7. _____ Has traveled to another country.

8. _____ Drives a foreign car.

9. _____ Speaks or understands a foreign language.

10. _____ Has relatives abroad.

Activity 18-3: LAND VALUE

Skills. Creating a graph from statistical material

Materials. Table of Iowa farmland values (in text)

Procedure

1. Review with students the recent trends in the agricultural community; e.g., individual farms have gradually increased in size, the number of farms has gradually declined, and the size of machinery has generally increased.

2. Examine the table of Iowa farmland values (in text). Have students research to complete the data for the current year. Next provide the class with grid paper to make a graph of trends in land values.

3. Conclude the lesson by discussing the following questions:

    a. What would farmers likely do as the value of their land increased rapidly?
      -They might sell, making the size of farms larger.
      -They might borrow from a bank, using their land as collateral, to expand their holdings.
    b. If farmers borrowed against their land and land values fell, what might result?
      -Banks might suffer because of the declining value of farmers' collateral compared to their loans.
      -It might become more difficult to borrow money.
      -Farmers might lose their property in foreclosures.

Activity 18-4: EROSION IN IOWA

Skills. Reading a political cartoon

Materials. *Des Moines Register* cartoon of soil erosion (in text)

Procedure

1. Introduce the lesson by discussing the importance of Iowa's rich soil to the economy of the state.

2. Use the following questions to discuss the cartoon:

    a. What problem is this cartoon illustrating?
      -Soil erosion
    b. Why is an hourglass used?
      -Time is running out on this problem.
    c. What is depicted in the top of the hourglass?
      -The earth

d. Why is the earth depicted in the top of the hourglass?
   -There is a double meaning here. Not only will the earth (or soil) be destroyed, our civilization as we know it will be undermined with the decline of agricultural resources.

3. Conclude the lesson by discussing current practices used in Iowa to conserve the soil.